COUNSELING IS LIKE . . .

The use of analogies in counseling

by

Margaret Ross

Printed in Victoria, Canada

National Library of Canada Cataloguing in Publication Data

Ross, Margaret, 1927-
        Counseling is like... : the use of analogies in counseling / written by Margaret Ross.
Includes bibliographical references.
ISBN 1-4120-0526-4
        I. Title.
LB1027.5.R68 2003   371.4   C2003-903300-7

TRAFFORD

This book was published on-demand in cooperation with Trafford Publishing.
On-demand publishing is a unique process and service of making a book available for retail sale to the public taking advantage of on-demand manufacturing and Internet marketing. On-demand publishing includes promotions, retail sales, manufacturing, order fulfilment, accounting and collecting royalties on behalf of the author.

Suite 6E, 2333 Government St., Victoria, B.C. V8T 4P4, CANADA
Phone   250-383-6864   Toll-free   1-888-232-4444 (Canada & US)
Fax   250-383-6804   E-mail   sales@trafford.com
Web site   www.trafford.com   TRAFFORD PUBLISHING IS A DIVISION OF TRAFFORD HOLDINGS LTD.
Trafford Catalogue #03-0895   www.trafford.com/robots/03-0895.html

10   9   8   7   6   5   4   3   2

ACKNOWLEDGMENTS

In many ways I feel that everyone with whom I have been in contact has played a role in the writing of this book. The contents came out of my life experiences which encouraged and supported me in my creative development.

Since it is not possible to name all those people, there are some special ones who deserve to be recognized.

Lucinda Pyatt spent several hours helping me to get organized and helped some of the writing, especially chapters 1 & 2 and the analogy, "Aladdin."

Jill Benton was a valuable sounding board for me. She also helped critique my analogies and contributed ideas for others.

Lyle and Susan Eide fed into my creative juices as I talked with them during my summer teaching at the University of Manitoba.

My many colleagues around the country who took the time to read my ideas several years ago and who encouraged me to write this book.

Dan Jones, former Director of Admissions at Marietta College, who first suggested a newsletter which would be sent to high school counselors. Thus the **EXPANDER** was born, which provided an outlet for my first analogies.

Sally Schafer is a proofreader extraordinaire, who not only proofread this book, but also proofread the **EXPANDER** for 10 years.

Penny Passavant who helped me to unravel the mysteries of the computer.

The Writers Group of Marietta College who gave me feedback as I struggled to edit the original manuscript.

The graphic illustration class of Marietta College who designed the cover of this book.

Last, and perhaps most important, is that unnamed student who first started me on the use of analogies some 32 years ago. Thanks also goes to the hundreds of students who followed me through my counseling office door and provided me the opportunity to grow as a person and as a counselor.

To all these and countless more, I owe my heartfelt thanks.

Margaret Ross

CONTENTS

III

V

INTRODUCTION

Analogies are a way of talking about experiences. We each experience life uniquely, so it is not possible to communicate identical interpretations of our experiences. Analogies help define our experiences to others by creating colored pictures. Like a collage, layers of meaning are built from expansion of the analogy in exploration of its likeness and dissimilarities to the experience being described.

WHY USE ANALOGIES FOR COUNSELING?

Several years ago when I first began counseling, I was working with a student who resisted the usual ways of approaching problems. Quite by accident, I used an analogy to explain a situation. It seemed as if what I had to say was not like "counseling" when put in the form of an analogy. She was more comfortable in accepting what I said. Since then I have used analogies with several students. My experience has been that I have been able to get students to consider possibilities through analogies they would otherwise not accept or even consider.

Many resistances are bypassed when you tell a story. Analogies develop a kind of story, a word-picture, if you will. The counselor can make contact with the student, a primary goal of counseling, through these creative encounters. As you are developing an analogy together, the counseling process unfolds in a way that is less threatening to the student. It allows the student more free thinking as your explore together where the idea may go. It allows you a broader range of ideas because you are not limited to "counselese" in either your mind or the student's.

Analogies offer possibilities that may not exist in the student's model of what counseling is. While experience is the best teacher, many experiences are not directly accessible to the student. Analogies, or storytelling, give access to those otherwise inaccessible experiences. For instance, as a midwestern child from the flat land, this author could experience, through a story having to pull hard against a long, uphill mountain track with <u>The Little Engine That Could</u>, chugging "I think I can, I think I can."

As children, we have all experienced through stories, myriad things that otherwise would not have been a part of our experience. Think about your favorite childhood stories, how real they became, and how they broadened your experience. As adults we can access through stories (analogies) in a similar way.

As adults we have an even greater ability to transfer several layers of meaning through symbolic experiencing. We can not only experience the straining against gravity as the train pulls up the difficult climb, we can explore the aspects of personal power, determination, and the power of a positive attitude as we read <u>The Little Engine That Could </u>to our children, and to ourselves.

Certainly an important reason for using the analogy format is that it is exciting. Working with analogies can be a freeing experience. Analogies can tap into collaborative creativity, an alive and enlivening process which experiments with possibilities. It is the actual <u>doing</u> part of creating personal growth or change. Working with analogies is fun! Using analogies generates energy in both the student and the counselor. In order to use the analogies to their fullest, it is important to allow the free-flow of ideas and opportunities for insight.

Analogy creation could be the practice or rehearsal for continued experimentation in the student's life. As counselors, we are asking people to engage in this very process in their lives outside the counseling room. Analogy construction is a cognitive/affective experience for both student and counselor for the purpose of gaining understanding about the student's life experiences. According to Rogers, (1951) one of the necessary and sufficient conditions for psychotherapeutic change is that the student feels understood by the counselor. Through the use of analogy the counselor can demonstrate this understanding.

Another important part of working with analogies is the present centeredness of the activity between two people. Even though they are talking metaphorically or symbolically about the past, they bring the past into the present by constructing the analogy in the present, with and between each other. This process is authentic. For Bugental, (1992) the number one goal of counseling is increased authenticity for the student.

WHAT ARE ANALOGIES?

The terms "analogy" and "metaphor" are often used interchangeably. Metaphor is defined as a figure of speech in which a word or phrase, literally denoting one kind of object or idea, is used in place of another to suggest a likeness or analogy between them, an implied comparison between two things unlike in most respects but alike in the respect in which they are compared. Analogy is defined as inference that if two or more things agree with one another, in some respects, they will probably agree in others.

The word itself is from the Greek <u>ana</u> <u>logon</u>, "according to a ration," and was used to mean similarity in proportional relationships, primarily geometric figures. The Greeks also used it to infer similarity of function. We use it today in the Miller Analogy Test (MAT): such as X is to Y, so A is to B, (You knew it was Greek to you, right!?)

For the purposes of this book we prefer Zinker's description: "a way of connecting things that aren't usually connected. Individuals can become connected through exploring (an analogy) because the new image appeals to them in different ways." (Zinker, pg. 170). Logical contradictions are sometimes the only way we have of defining our experience.

To share our experience with another is a challenge to our creativity. "Knowledge of," it seems, is distinctly different from "knowledge about." "Knowledge of" can be gained from reading and observation, from learning to speak the language. I can gain "knowledge about" the pain of dying by reading books on thanatology. However, "knowledge of" requires an inside view that comes from shared experience. This I can gain only through my own dying or by sharing through another, who can relate to me in some way, their experience.

Most other books dealing with metaphors in therapy, use the terms "therapist" and "client." In this book I have chosen to use the terms "counselor" and "student." The choice of these terms reflects the people for whom this book was written. The intended audience is public school counselors and/or college counselors. Counselors who work in these settings are usually involved in short term counseling. Many of the presenting issues in this setting deal with adolescent issues. The more seriously disturbed student is often beyond the training or purpose of counselors in school settings. It would be more appropriate for these students to seek out a therapist in a private setting or a mental health clinic.

CHAPTER 1

What are analogies? Why Analogies?

Why did I write this book? What purpose does it serve? There are already books that help us understand the significance of analogies and which teach us to use analogies. There are books that help us understand the significance of counseling theories and techniques which teach us how to practice counseling. The observation of techniques gives us an external view of how to use counseling techniques. In this book I strive to offer, through the use of analogies, a different view of counseling -- from the inside out.

    I started this book at the urging -- well, at least the encouragement-- of colleagues who had read some of my analogies and had used analogies in their own counseling. Some of the analogies included in this book have been developed from my own need to share the counseling experience with students and colleagues, others were developed at the request of colleagues who asked questions like: "How might I explain to the student their responsibility in counseling?" "How can I tell a student that not all dependency is unhealthy?"

or, "How do I explain that sometimes, before you get better you might hurt more?"

One of the things that I have found as I use analogies is that if the counselor has a germ of an idea on how to explore an issue with the student, then together the student and the counselor can develop a whole analogy. I think this is an important part of the concept. That is, the analogy is **not** the counselor's alone, but rather the student and counselor develop the analogy together through the process of collaborative creativity. This is why it is important to explore whether the mode of analogy is an appropriate one for this student. Some students are not comfortable working with analogies, so developing the analogy could indeed distract from the point you are trying to make as a counselor.

To experiment with a new counseling technique takes a certain amount of courage. You might think of it as learning how to cook. When I first started to cook I "did it by the book." As I became more experienced, I began to experiment a bit, to add a little bit more of this and not so much of that, until my creation, whatever it might be, became a reflection of my taste and personality. So it is with the use of analogies in counseling. To be most effective, the analogy should reflect the personality of both the student and the counselor.

If the counselor is rigidly narrow in the variety of techniques he or she will use, the students may not feel free to use the mode best suited to them if it does not fit the counselor's narrow restrictions. It is the counselor's responsibility to have the courage to experiment, and to allow his thoughts to be free, to flow, rather than to attempt to fit into some preconceived pattern.

In order to use analogies to their fullest, it is important to allow the free-flowing of ideas, to open up one's self to expanded opportunities for insight. Before you begin using analogies with students, it might be important to practice thinking in analogy format. There are at least two ways you can do this. One is that you read the following chapters while allowing your mind to be free to add to or change the analogies I have presented. There is no one right way for an analogy to develop. So if your thinking goes in a different direction than mine, that is not a problem. Rather it is an indication that you are plugged into your own creative thinking.

Another warm-up you might use is to imagine yourself as an object, a place, or an animal. Explore how you experience things as that object, place, or animal.

I am my study. I have the tools for work and objects for play. My closet shelves are loaded with both office supplies and games. I am seldom tidy, yet everything I have is accessible and often used.

Expand on the image for as long as it holds your interest. Bring other people, objects or animals into the imagery. What are the reactions--feelings, thoughts. When you have finished you have lived, at least for a few minutes and imagistically, inside the analogy. As you make statements about that object, place or animal, you gain new insights about yourself.

Of course, it isn't necessary to "live inside" an analogy for it to be useful. We seldom become that involved with the image itself. Part of our awareness, however, does enter into the analogy and opens up our field of experience, broadening our learning.

Remember, in using analogies it should always be possible to show that the similarities noted bear relevantly on the point to be made, whereas the differences are irrelevant. In working with the student it is important that they explain their own analogy. The student may have a completely different interpretation than you and that is all right. It is the student's analogy, not yours. I have found that, in working with students, sometimes my comments can be far off base, and still open open up new territory for us to explore.

The analogy format taps into the right brain, bringing with the word pictures a vast wealth of associations from our often neglected creative reservoir. In teaching workshops in creativity, I find that many people doubt their own creativity. When we move beyond the realm of art and music, the students are often surprised at how creative they can be. And they enjoy it. This combination of right and left brain function greatly enlarges the student's ability for self-help.

SUGGESTIONS FOR USING ANALOGIES

a. Keep the analogy brief. Expanded too much, the analogy can become a burden or a distraction. Keep bringing the analogy back to the issue being addressed. Yet don't be too rigid in this. Part of the value of the analogy is an indirect approach to what may be a sensitive area for the student. Keep an awareness of the student's involvement with the image and trust your instincts about how much direct contact the image should have with the meaning.

b. Trust your student to find what he needs in the analogy. Given the freedom to find his own meaning, the student may discover treasures that neither of you expected from the analogy.

c. Draw on your own instincts of how and when to use an analogy. You will need to experiment with this. As the counselor, it is important to draw from your own life experiences as you work with analogies. When you use your own experiences, you will find that the ideas will flow more easily. Preplanning results or formalizing interpretations may inhibit the energy and creativity you and your student both need to find creative solutions.

d. Trust the process of the unconscious, your's and your student's. "The Answer" may not evolve out of the analogy, at least not immediately. Allow the analogy to be a seed that may need time to gestate.

e. Respond within the analogy, addressing the multiple levels of the images. It is not necessary to bring every meaning in the analogy to the conscious level. The images are there for later use, when appropriate.

f. Listen to the unconscious in your student's analogies. It is not necessary to interpret every word and symbol. It is more important to get a sense of the whole of the student's imagery. Are the symbols heavy? light? colorful? dull? small? large? etc.? What is the analogy saying beneath the surface?

g. Reinforce the student's use of analogy without regard to the content. There is no wrong analogy. Every image the student uses has meaning for the student, even if you don't "see" that meaning yourself.

h. Pace the analogy to the tone/mood/pace of the student. The student's involvement with the development of the analogy is important to its efficacy. The student may be involved in the creation of the images/analogy or the student may merely be involved as a listener and respondent. Ideally, the student will participate in discovering the likenesses and dissimilarities within the analogy.

i. Go slowly enough to encourage participation. Allow silences. There is power in silences.

j. Include sensory detail. An image that can be accessed sensually is stronger and will "hook" the imagination more quickly.

k. Watch for unconscious responses to the story: changes in breathing, posture, facial expression. Reinforce desired changes. Engage the student's creative energies through these responses.

l. Enjoy. This kind of work can be fun and energizing for both of you.

Of course, not all students work well with analogies, and analogies are not appropriate all of the time. It is necessary for the counselor to explore with the student to see whether or not they can work well with analogies.

Right now I need to warn you about THE LAW OF THE HAMMER. It is: Give a kid a hammer and everything in sight will need to be pounded . While I can't tell you WHEN to use an analogy, I can offer some guidelines.

1. If you have a student who has difficulty expressing herself, many times the introduction of an analogy makes it

easier for the student to talk.

2. When you have trouble understanding what the student is trying to tell you, an analogy can make this clearer.

3. Use sparingly.   While the purpose of this book is to explore the use of analogies in counseling, it is important to make sure you use other techniques as well. Your total counseling session should not consist of only analogies.

4. Tune into the student's involvement. Is creating the analogy more exciting to you than to the student?

Following is one example of how you might develop analogy with a student. (CO, counselor, ST, student.)

CO: Hi, what can I do for you today?

ST: I don't like the major I'm in, but I don't know what to do about it?

CO: Tell me more.

ST: Well, I'm not sure what I want to do, but I do know that I don't want the major I have.

CO: Explain that a little more . . . .

ST: I was good in this subject in high school, but now I'm having a lot of trouble with it in college. I feel I'm up against a brick wall.

CO: What does the wall look like to you?

ST: Well, I can't seem to see over it and there are no doors or windows--it is solid.
CO: What does that mean to you?
ST: I'm blocked. I never considered doing anything else and now that I'm having trouble with the subject, I don't know what to do.
CO: How wide is the wall?
ST: I don't know. I've never looked to the side, only straight ahead.
CO: Take a moment and see if you can figure out how wide the wall it.
ST: O.K. . . . . When I reach out, I can feel the side.
CO: Explore that some more and see what might be there for you.
ST: I guess moving sideways to look at something else, doesn't mean I've failed.

Here you have a place to encourage the student to keep looking. Another option is to talk about the student's concept of failure. There are other avenues you could explore. The key is to throw one out and see where the student takes it.

Now it is time to begin doing, to move from learning of to learning about. I wish you excitement, growth, life, and, most of all, fun!

CHAPTER 2

How to develop analogies

In the following chapters I have given you samples of many different types of analogies. My purpose is to demonstrate that any topic is fair game for an analogy. Your only limitation is your own imagination. Remember there is no WRONG way to develop an analogy.

When you are developing an analogy, it is important to allow the analogy to belong to the student. I remember once when I was working with a student I used the metaphor, "Well, I guess your chickens have come home to roost." He looked at me with a blank stare and finally said, "I don't have the slightest idea of what you are talking about.!" This is an example of my introducing an analogy about which the student had no knowledge of the contents. Obviously, the student needs to relate to the analogy in some way.

The students take what they know and, through analogy, represent the situation in terms of their own experiences. By allowing the students to introduce the concept, you are then in the position of helping the students explore <u>their</u> <u>own</u> analogy. In working with the analogy, the counselor must also be careful not to introduce new concepts. This can be avoided by asking the students questions about their analogy.

Many people use analogies without being aware that that is what they are doing. If you listen to everyday speech, you will find most people using analogies to describe a situation, how they feel, or what they want to do. Gentner and Holyoak (1997) talk about the "illusion of familiarity" which depends on the power of the human mind to find similarities between past experiences and the present situation. This allows students a way of understanding an unfamiliar situation in terms of a situation that is already familiar. When the student presents the analogy, it is important that each person significantly involved in the student's problem is represented in the analogy's cast of characters.

As a counselor, you get your cues for using analogies from the people with whom you are working. For example, someone may say, "I feel like I'm hitting a brick wall." or, "She treats me like a maid," or, "I feel like I'm drowning." You then are in a position to explore what this means to the individual. It is important not to project what this phrase means to you--let the student give meaning. In the final resolution, the student determines the desired outcome. When this has been demonstrated, the counselor's role is to help the student develop a strategy to reach that outcome, if it can be reached.

A critical factor in the outcome is that it must be something over which the student has control. For example, students can control their reaction to a specific situation. They can not control the behavior of another person. Gordon (1978) suggests that a metaphor which satisfies the basic requirement of being structurally equivalent with the situation and provides a workable resolution can not only be effective, it may also be sufficient.

In *Distinctive Therapeutic Uses of Metaphor b*y Cirillo and Crider (1995), an example is given of a man describing his wife as a rock and she talks of her husband as a door. After the husband and wife explore the surface meaning of the analogies, the counselor then helps them explore the positive aspects of these metaphors. This opens up a whole area of understanding between the two people.

Let us say we were going to develop an analogy about "showing your own home movie." The counselor might ask the following questions: What does the movie look like to you? Is there anything you would like to change in your movie? Would you like to change the ending? What would it look like? What would it take to do this? Depending on the student's responses, other questions related to the responses might be asked.

After exploring these aspects, the counselor is in the position to encourage the student to take this analogy a step further and relate it to the current issue(s) with which the student is dealing. That is, it is helpful to transform the analogy to create change or a solution. The analogies in the following chapters will illustrate this point.

Kopp and Craw (1998) suggest the following interview protocol for exploring and transforming client-generated metaphors.

STEP 1--Notice metaphors!

STEP 2--"When you say [the metaphor) what image or picture comes to mind?" or, ". . what image or picture do you see in your mind's eye?" or, "What does the (metaphor] look like?"

STEP 3--Explore the metaphor as a sensory image.:

a. Setting (e.g., "What else do you see?" or, "Describe the scene or an aspect of the scene [associated with

the metaphoric image]")
b. Action/interaction (e.g., "What else is going on in the metaphoric image])?" or, "What are the other people [in the metaphoric image} saying/thinking/doing?")
c. Time (e,.g., "What led up to this?", "What was happening [just] before [the situation in the metaphor]?", "What happens next?")
STEP 4--"What is it like to be [the metaphoric image]?" or "What is your experience of [the metaphoric image]?" or, "What are you feeling as you [the metaphoric image]?"
STEP 5--The therapist (counselor) says, " If you could change the image in any way, how would you change it?"
STEP 6--"What connections (parallels) do you see between your image of [the metaphoric image] and [the original situation]?"
STEP 7--"How might the way you changed the image apply to your current situation?" (p. 310-311)

Counselors, in contrast to therapists, are mostly involved in short term therapy. This term has many interpretations, but the usual one is that this means twelve or fewer

21

counseling sessions. The use of analogies helps move this process along in a way that is meaningful to students.

It is hypothesized that the process of shifting between their explored and transformed metaphoric imagery and their current life problem creates the potential for new insights into the name of the problem and new possibilities for constructive problem-solving. (Kopp & Craw, 1998).

How to use this book.

As you peruse this book, I hope that it will help you to think about counseling in new ways--to develop a mind set for analogies. I also hope that the content of the analogies will aid you in working with your students.

A word of caution. You need to be careful not to get so involved in the analogy that you forget the purpose of it.

It is important you do not force the use of an analogy. To be helpful, the analogy must be natural and grow out of your work together. The student needs to be part of the process.

CHAPTER 3

The Art of Counseling

I have organized the following chapters, according to topics. Some analogies could well be under a different chapter and that is O.K. The important thing is to be aware of the analogies and how you might grow and learn from them. Enjoy!

THE ART OF COUNSELING

According to *Webster's New World Dictionary,* one definition of art is "the human ability to make things; creativity of man (woman) as distinguished from the world of nature. Creative work or its principles; making or doing of things that display form, beauty, and unusual perception." Surely, within this definition is the art of counseling and the use of analogies to express that art. There is a grace and beauty in the counseling process where the student and the counselor interact in such a way "that displays form, beauty, and unusual perception."

Counseling is like...Working a jigsaw puzzle.

When students first come to counseling they are unsure of how the process works. They know they are there to talk about what is bothering them. What they are unsure of is how much they should tell. They want to talk about the issues, but often times are unclear as to how much detail to give. Many are concerned about "not wasting" the counselor's time with seemingly unrelated information.

As a way of helping the students understand that it is important to give information and not withhold what they deem as unimportant, I use the analogy of working a jigsaw puzzle. This analogy helps them understand that they are not always the best judge of what is important in understanding the issues they bring to counseling. It also helps the students to understand that something that seems unrelated to their issues might be a key to understanding. Only when we have all the information available are we then able to discern what is important and what is not important.

Counseling can be compared to putting together a jigsaw puzzle. In both instances the purpose is to take many different shapes and put them together in some order to "make sense" out of the things.

When putting together a jigsaw puzzle, there are a variety of approaches. No one can say one method is better than the other. Rather, method is a matter of preference. So it is with counseling. One counselor will use approach "A," another approach "B,"and so on. The end goal remains the same, making sense out of the many pieces . . getting a clear picture to "solve" the puzzle.

One of the major ways counseling differs from working a jigsaw puzzle is that the counselor is totally dependent on the student to furnish the pieces. For puzzles, it is a matter of opening a box, turning out all the pieces, sorting them out in whatever manner you choose, and putting the puzzle together. Counseling, on the other hand, relies on the ability and judgment of the student to furnish the pieces and to do this in such a way that the counselor is able to recognize these pieces.

Involved in this recognition is the skill of the student to articulate what is going on within. Herein lies a problem. If, for example, the student has been told that this color is "brown," but when the student comes into counseling and the counselor says, "What you have been taught is 'brown' is really 'green'."

How does the student deal with this? Who is to be believed? While the student might wish to believe the counselor that the color is "green," how do you reconcile the fact that others have named the color "brown."

When putting together the puzzle, a helpful approach is to put the border together first. While doing the border, if the student gives you a middle piece, obviously it won't "fit." When this happens, it is important not to reject the piece and say it doesn't belong. Rather, it is necessary to patiently keep the piece available, so that when you and the student begin to fill in the puzzle, the piece is available.

When I work a puzzle I need to try out pieces several times. Sometimes I try to put the pieces in too soon and they don't fit. Sometimes I need to turn the pieces around until they fit. All of this takes patience and time. An attempt to force a piece where it doesn't belong could change the student's puzzle.

Another problem is that many times the student is unable to recognize what may be important. If the student considers something unimportant, it may be difficult for the counselor to become aware of that piece. As in a jigsaw puzzle, all pieces are important, large and small, the "small" connecting pieces as well as the "'big" pieces. If the student provides only those pieces deemed "important," it leaves the counselor with the task of trying to put together the puzzle with several pieces missing. The student, on the other hand, becomes frustrated because the "big" pieces were presented and nothing seems to happen. When this occurs, the student becomes discouraged, not understanding that, as in a jigsaw puzzle, you can't put the puzzle together with only the large pieces. Often the "small" pieces turn out to be the more important ones in the connecting process.

Because "jigsaw counseling" depends so much on the student's perceptions, other problems occur. For example, from the student's point of view, when he/she says something is "red," the student may not realize that all that is given is a color. To work a puzzle, you also need the shape. Or when the opposite happens, the shape is given and not the color. While it is not an impossible situation and, if you work long enough, the process of elimination will put these pieces in the appropriate places, it would be more helpful if more complete information were available.

Jigsaw counseling is further complicated

by the fact that neither the student nor the counselor knows how big the puzzle is. It could be a 500 piece, a 25 piece, or even a 1000 piece puzzle. It is difficult then to put a time limit on the process of putting together the picture.

Also, since the student has many puzzles within, it is not always clear if the piece presented belongs to the puzzle you are working on or some other puzzle. Therefore, it is necessary to put out as many pieces as possible. The task of the student and counselor working together is to figure out if a particular piece "fits." Because of this, it is better to have "too many" pieces than to hold some back.

As parts of the puzzle begin to come together, the puzzle becomes more real. This very "realness" becomes a problem for some students. One can expect that some of the parts could be ugly. This does not necessarily mean that the total picture will be ugly. However, because neither the student, nor the counselor can see the total picture, the student often fears that when all the ugly parts are put together, the total picture will be so ugly it will be overwhelming. Therefore, the student often presumes that it is easier to manage several small "ugly" parts than one huge ugly picture.

The role of the counselor, in supporting and encouraging the student at this step, is crucial. From past experience, the counselor knows that the student will be able to handle the completed puzzle. In fact, the very act of completing the puzzle gives the student strength. When you can name the unknown, make it "real," it often becomes manageable, because the student now knows just what has to be dealt with. One of the ways in which the counselor can teach the student, to help herself, is to encourage the sharing of those parts of the puzzle she has begun to put together on her own . Together they can work to solidify the total picture, even though these may be considered by the student to be "ugly," fearful parts. This is the point at which the student must have faith in the counselor - to be there - to be supportive - to be non judgmental - to care. It is under these conditions that the student dares to take the risk of putting the pieces together and to look at the total picture.

The active participation of the student is essential. As the counselor, I don't know what the picture looks like. I depend on the student for that. I don't know when the puzzle is done. The student knows that. It is his/her picture.

The student   will know when the puzzle is complete and is meaningful. It is the student's puzzle. The counselor's role is to support the effort to put it together, not to create a new puzzle. It is a special moment when together you know that the pieces fit and the total picture makes sense to the student.

Counseling is like . . . Building a fire.

Some students, when they come into counseling the first time, want to unload everything they have been carrying around. This is a sensitive time. It could have taken the student several weeks to get up the courage to come in and once in my office, there is a need to unload everything at once. The danger of this of course, is that the student becomes overwhelmed with all the information and then clams up. At the same time, it is important not to shut the student down by stopping them in the middle of his story. The way I work with this situation is to allow the student to unload the story, then I will use the analogy of building a fire to help the student understand that we can't deal with everything at once. We need to put some of the information aside, build a foundation, and then begin to add information as it seems appropriate. Because the student has given me the full load, I have some background and can begin to know when to feed in information the student gave me in the first part of the session.

In the last several days, I have had an occasion to build a fire in my fireplace. What I became aware of is that I started the fire with several small pieces of wood. When the fire "got going," I added a larger log. If I put on too big a log, the fire could smother and go out. To keep this from happening, from time to time, I would feed smaller logs to the fire. It was also important to make sure the air circulated to keep the fire burning.

I am also aware that there is a time to let the fire go out. It would not be appropriate to put on several logs just before you wanted to let the fire go out.

In this vein, I started thinking about counseling. Usually you start out with less significant information. As the student "gets going", larger and larger issues arise. Because things are moving along, sometimes we can lose sight of the big issue which might shut the student down. The student could get smothered or overwhelmed. When this happens, our job is to make sure the student comes up for air so that the student can keep going.

What this requires of us, as counselors, is to keep an awareness, as best we can, of how "loaded up" the student is. We can't always know this, since we have no idea of the magnitude of the issue for the student. What we can do, is to be aware of when the student is "grasping for air" and to help get some "life" into the fire so that the student can keep on going.

Occasionally, it might be appropriate for the fire to die out and to be relit at another time. We need to make sure that neither the student nor the counselor, adds fuel just before the end of the session. In this case, the "fuel" could be in the form of new issues and/or heavy emotions.

COUNSELING is like ....Making a print.

When a student tells you their story, the counselor accepts it at face value. At the same time it is helpful to be tuned into what might develop as the story unfolds. I have found, that for many students, it is easier to start out with something that is not bothering them very much, to experience a sense of what counseling might be for them. This is a time when the student experiences the person in the counselor and determines if this is someone with whom they wish to work. Many times as the student becomes more comfortable the story will change and incorporate many things that were not apparent in the original story.

The analogy of making a print from a negative expresses this phenomenon as it relates to counseling.

In recent years I have developed and nurtured an interest in black and white photography. It occurred to me the other day, when I was working in the dark room, that printmaking is a lot like counseling.

Let me tell you about what is, at this point in time, my favorite print. I took the photo on a bright October day while canoeing with a friend on the Little Hocking River. Where we go, the river is a result of the backwater of the Ohio River, which means that it is shallow, so that we never see motor boats or other people. On this day, we were slowly going up the river, when I spotted a dead tree hanging over the river. The tree was full of Pileated woodpecker holes (for the non-birder, "Woody Woodpecker" is a caricature of a Pileated woodpecker). As we approached the tree, I took pictures from several angles focusing totally on the holes. When I started doing test strips in the dark room, I was aware of some other things on the paper, but didn't pay much attention to them. My first full sized print revealed, not just the reflection on the water of the tree I had focused on, but also the reflection of the whole woods. Since there were no leaves on the trees I had these "ghost" reflections in the river--exciting!

Relating this reflection to counseling, sometimes when we work with a student we tend to get focused on the "main event" and don't really take into our awareness what else might be there. If we spend all our time on this main focus, we will miss the other parts of the individual and loose out on the complete picture of the person with whom we are working. As with printmaking, it is important to do our "test strips" and then work up the full sized picture to see what else might be there. When I make a print, I may make 10 or 12 before I have the one with which I am really pleased. A part of the picture which was originally background when the picture was shot may become an interesting focal point when it is discovered in the printmaking process. The picture offers many intricacies in its wholeness, if we take the time to investigate the subtleties. We may need to go back time after time, to nurture one aspect or another, in order to get the final picture. When we take the time and patience to do this, photography is very exciting.

I believe that this same principle applies in working with a student. What seems to be apparent in our first encounter may change many times before our work is done. Through the use of creative collaboration, we may discover some of the background which becomes important in the developing of the student to her full potential.

Every time I go into the dark room, I learn more about myself and what I am doing. Every time I work with a student, I learn more about myself, as well as about what I am doing. Neither printmaking nor counseling can be rushed and we must be open to learning every time we enter the process.

Counseling is like ....Taking a trip.

To help a student understand what the counseling process is like, I use the analogy of taking a trip. For many students, counseling will be a new experience and they are not quite sure how it works. The analogy of taking a trip helps them to appreciate what the counselor-student relationship is and how the two interact. It can also help set the stage for the ending of counseling.

I recently took an extended trip and while we were traveling along , it occurred to me how much taking a trip was like counseling.

On my trip, I was with a number of people, most of whom I did not know, and many I would have no history with after the trip was over. Because of this, it was important to get acquainted so that the trip was comfortable, but not important to share our complete histories with each other. The acquainting period lasted over time and there were some people I shared more history with than others.

Because we were traveling in a foreign country I heard many things I did not understand. Some of this was due to the language barrier and some of it was due to the fact that I didn't have the history to appreciate all that I saw. In our group, there were 42 people who came from different parts of the United States with different backgrounds. This meant that we had many different points of reference. What one person might be interested in pursuing, others were not. If this were to be a pleasant trip, then we had to learn to accommodate each other's needs and desires.

We traveled by bus, which meant that on some days we had to travel a long time and distance to get to the interesting parts of the country. There were times when I questioned if the energy involved was worth the destination. However, when we reached the destination, it was usually worth the trip.

As we traveled through the countryside our guide did his best to give us a history of our destination so we could better appreciate what it was we were going to see. Since this country was all new to me, it really helped me to understand why we went where we did.

In the course of our trip we traveled back and forth between time zones and had to adjust our watches along the way. We also had to accept the fact, that just because we wore watches, it did not mean that we were in control of when things would happen.

When we had some time to poke around on our own, there were many things we wanted to do. We learned early on that we couldn't do it all and if we were going to do anything, it was important to pick and choose that which we thought would be most interesting to us and our particular tastes.

At the end of our time together, it was important to say our goodbyes and bring closure to the experience. This allowed us to set aside this special time together and have good memories about it and move on with our lives after the trip.

When the student first comes to counseling, there is a period of time in which you get acquainted. Not only do you learn each other's name, but also a little bit about each other. In the process of counseling you may hear many things you don't understand. Partly because you and the student have a different point of reference.

The more you are with each other, the more you begin to understand and you build a foundation made up of the history you begin to develop together. In some cases it is necessary to spend a considerable amount of time together sharing this history before you get to the basic issue(s) the student wishes to bring forth. There have been times when, at this stage, I have wondered where this was going. If I am patient and allow the student the space to explore, there is usually a purpose to the path the student has chosen.

In the case of counseling, the counselor acts as the guide along the way. The guide's job is to help the student see the interesting or important parts and to help the student pick and choose. Sometimes a lot of information is presented before the reason for coming evolves. The student needs to be made aware that you can't do it all, and that you don't need to do it all at one time. In the case of counseling, it is possible to return to continue the journey.

There may also be the need to adjust time schedules as to when something will get done. It is not unusual for the counselor and the student to be on different time schedules. In most cases, it is the job of the counselor to adjust the time schedule to the student's.

After you have "visited" one place, you and the student may move on to another point of interest, or the student may decide to say goodbye and move on, maybe to return later. Unlike a trip which has a definite ending, it is sometimes hard to determine when this time comes in counseling. Some students try to postpone it, while others want to cut it short. The counselor's job is to help the student see that there is "life outside of counseling" and to close the relationship in such a way that the student will be comfortable coming back, if that is appropriate.

Counseling is like....Walking the dogs.

In the best of all worlds, when a student comes in for counseling, the student and counselor work together along the same path. However, this does not always happen. To help explain to the student what can happen, I use the analogy of walking the dogs. This helps the student to understand that sometimes we get away from the issue at hand, and that both of us need to focus on keeping on the track. I also believe that under certain circumstances it is O.K. for the student to take what I might think of as a side journey. Often times this proves to be significant. The walking of the dogs analogy also helps remind me that I need to monitor my work to make sure I am not the one going off on a tangent.

Friends of mine have two Corgis. Their leashes come together into one that the owner holds. When they take the dogs out, sometimes one dog will head off in a different direction and that drags the second dog off in the same direction. Sometimes, one dog will just stop and refuse to go on and that means the second dog has to stop too. Fortunately, most of the time, the dogs walk together and don't pull on each other.

It struck me that this is what can happen in counseling. Sometimes the student will head off in a direction and before the counselor realizes it, the counselor is following along and they are off on a tangent, away from the issue under consideration. I have been in the situation where the student just stops and I become aware that I am doing all the work!

On the other hand, I have been in a counseling situation where the student goes on nonstop and it has been necessary for me to help the student pause and spend some time in reflection.

Then there are those moments when we are both working together, going in the same direction, and the process is moving forward more smoothly.

It is necessary for the counselor to be sensitive to what is happening. Sometimes it is necessary for the student to take what seems like a divergent path. And, we need to be aware that what seems like a tangent doesn't always end up going in another direction. It is important that, within the framework, the student is given the freedom to go down another avenue. I can recall when that "other avenue" often led to the real issue at hand.

I have also been in the situation where it was important for the student to "unload everything" before focus could be attained. Again, as the counselor, we must not stop the student too soon. The risk would be that the student would stop and not start again.

To me this is where the ART of counseling comes in.   The counselor and the student are linked in a common endeavor like the two-dog leash. The "art" is in keeping up with, or on the same path as the student, so the student isn't yanked to a halt or off his unique path. The counselor is responsible for smooth accompaniment or pace. The counselor has to be alert to what is on the student's path so that they may pursue it together.

Counseling is like . . . A stack of salad plates.

Often times I encounter a student in counseling who becomes very frustrated because once they deal with an issue, another one just as important seems to pop up. In using the analogy of a stack of salad plates, the student can begin to appreciate that often times there is more than one issue that needs attention. It also helps the student appreciate that not all issues need to be dealt with at the same time. Some are "hot" issues, that is to say, current and pressing. Others may be "cold" issues. Something that happened in the past that doesn't need to be addressed now or perhaps it may never need to be addressed. Time and growth will determine which is which.

Salad bars are very popular in many restaurants today. The usual setup is to have a system where the plates are dispensed one at a time. As the top plate is removed, the stack moves up so that a plate is ready for the next customer.

In a lot of ways counseling is like this. Often a student comes in with what appears to be one thing to talk about and, as we start talking about it, other issues come to the top. I think it is important to help students become aware of this possibility so that they don't panic and begin to feel as though their lives are coming apart when this happens.

As with the stack of plates, there is no way of knowing ahead of time how many layers are there. Sometimes it might be one or two. At other times there could be many more. One of the things I help students appreciate is that, like the salad bar, it is possible to go back. In other words, everything that surfaces doesn't need to be dealt with all at once. Most salad bars have a great diversity of items to choose from. And, indeed, you must make a choice. There is such a thing as piling the salad too high and having it fall off the plate. Another phenomenon in the analogy is that when we go back to the salad bar, we take a clean plate. This can also be true in counseling. It is not always necessary, or desirable, to carry over an issue. Sometime it is best to start with a clean plate. If appropriate, we can pull all the issues together at a later date.

Another characteristic of salad bars is that sometimes the plates are warm and sometimes they are cold. That is to say, some student issues may demand more immediate attention. I also believe that some of the issues that come to the top are "cold" in the sense that they have been around a long time. These "cold" issues may still need to be dealt with without the pressure of "now." In my work I may encounter, let's say, a freshman and we will deal with the "hot" issues, and in the process become aware of some of the "cold" issues. The student may choose to come back a year or more later to talk about them rather than taking on all issues at once. It is also true that sometimes before you get to the bottom of the stack of plates, someone comes along and puts more plates on the stack. This is especially true of college-aged students who are maturing through a multitude of new experiences in a short period of time. I think that may also be true of counseling issues. Just about the time we might think we have resolved the issues, something happens to add more on. My own experience of this is called "growth." I think that part of living and growing is that we never get everything resolved. Nor is that even desirable.

COUNSELING IS LIKE...Working with the trunk of a tree.

When you see a tree in the woods most of us just see a tree. It can be tall or short, smooth or gnarled, fat or skinny. At this stage it is hard to imagine what the beauty captured inside might be.

When the tree trunk is viewed by an artist, she begins to see the potential. Even then, the potential is not seen until somehow the trunk is opened up. I'm told by artists who work in wood that before they make the first cut, they live with the trunk for a while and study it to see what might be revealed. The artist has no preconceived idea of what might be hidden in the wood. Rather she waits for the wood to reveal itself. She lets the grain and coloration dictate the work to unfold. To not wait, the wrong cut may spoil the creation hidden inside. I know artists who may have a piece of wood in their studio a long time before they work on it.

This is a lot like counseling. When a student comes to you, you have no idea of what might be inside. It is important to wait for the student to reveal what is there. The counselor may have some preconceived ideas based on experience. To act on these ideas would be a disservice to the student. The counselor needs to spend time with the student, providing a nurturing environment so that the student feels free to reveal what is inside. Beginning counselors like to ask questions. What they get in return is the answer to the questions, but not necessarily why the student came. As with the tree trunk, sometimes the beauty is not revealed at the first encounter. It may be necessary to provide time for the outer protective layers to be sloughed off, so that the real beauty, the core if you will, can be revealed. The student may not be ready the first time she comes to see you. Sometimes a student will come, only to disappear and maybe return two or three months later or even a year later.

With many students, others have acted too soon or have not appreciated the hidden beauty. Often times a scar is left rather than a way of opening. The counselor's job is to provide the time and space for the student to heal from these scars. When that has taken place, then the student will feel more comfortable allowing the outer protective layer to fall off. The student begins to unfold and the hidden beauty will be revealed. Unlike the tree trunk the student may continue to grow and develop. Counseling is an art and the counselor is the artist, looking for the beauty.

CHAPTER 4

COUNSELOR GROWTH

One can not grow in a vacuum. What helps us to grow and learn about ourselves is the interaction we have with others. I know that when I am counseling I get as much from the counseling session as does the student. If I don't , I wonder if I were *really* present. Many of the analogies in this section involve the interaction between counselor and student.

Counseling is like . . . Turning a kaleidoscope.

I have had 25 years of experience as a counselor in a college counseling center. This means that I basically worked with young people between the ages of 18 and 22. In this stage of their growth, they shared many common problems. In essence, I had heard them all. But had I? I needed to be careful to respect the issues of the individual student and to hear the individual pain. Just because the story was the same didn't mean the situation was. To help me (and you) keep this in perspective, I offer the analogy of turning a kaleidoscope. I would even suggest that you get one for your office and in between appointments, take a few minutes to play with it. This will do at least two things: remind you of the differences between the students you see and also relax you so that you will be fresh to meet your next appointment.

I collect kaleidoscopes and have several different types, styles and formats. Some are small and others are large, but they also have some characteristics in common. Kaleidoscopes basically work on the same principles. You must move them in some way to get results. Something else I have noticed about them, is that regardless of the type, over time most of them will repeat a pattern. The patterns produced are different among the kaleidoscopes, but sooner or later, the same pattern will emerge within each of the kaleidoscopes. Some patterns are more beautiful than others. Some are more complicated. These characteristics remind me of the students with whom we work. They are unique individuals. All are different in many ways, but there is usually a common theme that emerges. This is both a blessing and a curse. The blessing is that we have been there before in this situation and know that the students can emerge from it. The curse is that if we are not careful we can become complacent about what the students are struggling with and be tempted to give them answers that worked for others. In my 25 years as a college counselor, I have heard the same stories over and over. I need to remind myself that even though the stories are the same, the students are different. Their individual pain is unique to them and I must be careful to respect the integrity of each student.

How do we work to stay fresh and not fall into poor attitudes about the students? I believe this is where we must continue to be involved in our own professional growth, whether through reading, talking with colleagues, going to conferences or taking workshops. Successful counselors use kaleidoscope thinking. Do what a kaleidoscope does by taking a new perspective or angle on the problems everyone else sees--shaking up the pieces, challenging assumptions and getting a new set of possibilities.

We also need to be aware of what is going on in our own lives. We need to keep our personal issues out of the counseling office. In my career I have had the occasion to teach counseling practicum. One of the biggest challenges I had to deal with in beginning counselors was to help them keep their psychological distance from the issues being presented to them.

Counseling is like . . . Packing your own chute.

Depending on where they did their training, counselors can be exposed to many different theories on how to be a counselor. Often times this becomes very confusing. Yet at the same time it can be very helpful. Hopefully, the training was done in a setting where counselors were encouraged to try out many different approaches to counseling to see what seems to fit them best.

I believe that one of the more important elements in the counseling situation is the person who is the counselor and what his personal philosophy of counseling might be. Through the practice of a variety of theories of counseling, the counselor can find the theory that seems to fit with his personal philosophy. The counselor must do more than imitate what he has been exposed to. It is important that the counselor trust himself and believe in what and how he is practicing the art of counseling.

The analogy of packing your own chute addresses the issue of counselors trusting themselves as they work with students. A belief in what they are doing is the best way for counselors to function. Not all counselors have the same theory and that is O.K. The key is for the counselor to trust himself to work in the way that fits best.

An experienced skydiver likes to pack his own chute. However, it takes hours of jumping and practice before the jumper has the knowledge to pack a parachute. When a jumper is putting his life in that little pack on the back, he wants to make sure that the parachute has been packed correctly. There needs to be the confidence that when the cord is pulled, the 'chute will open and result in a safe landing.

I'm told that when people are first learning how to jump, they like to have a more experienced person pack the 'chute--one who knows from experience how to fold the chute so that it works properly. As a person gains experience in jumping, there comes a time when the jumper prefers to take over the responsibility of packing the 'chute.

I was thinking about this in relation to growing and it occurred to me that there is a parallel. That is to say, when we are young and inexperienced, we tend to depend on others to make decisions for us. In a sense, we let them pack our 'chute. Eventually, we begin to gain experience and confidence to the point of taking on more responsibility for ourselves. We begin to "pack our own 'chutes" with the experiences we have gained under the guidance of a significant other.

As we continue to grow, there comes a point when we make the decision to go solo--to pack our own 'chute and to have enough confidence in our skills that we are willing to pull the rip cord. Some are ready. On the other hand, there are some who are willing to pack the 'chute but do not have enough self-confidence in their own packing to pull the cord. In this critical situation, they fail to trust themselves and fall back on the "supervisor," be that a parent, spouse, or counselor.

Packing our own 'chute sometimes gets complicated when others may not want us to reach this stage of independence. By trying to control the packing of our 'chute, they can keep control of us. This makes it difficult, but not impossible, to grow up and out.

We all grow up with "shoulds" and "oughts." Packing our own 'chutes means looking at these rules and reevaluating them for ourselves. We may keep them all, or none, or some of them. In the end, what we do with the rules is our choice. We, not someone else, decides which ones to put in our 'chute. There comes a point in each of our lives, when we must make the hard decision--are we willing to step out on our own and pack our own 'chutes?

One of the implications of this is that we must be ready to break some ties with old relationships. It could mean giving up some security--to jump out on your own. It means, too, learning to live with and to appreciate one's self--a willingness to accept the consequences of our personal decisions, regardless of what those consequences might be.

And, we must be willing to let others pack their 'chutes. When we are involved with another we must be able to deal with them in a way that prepares them for the time when they pack their own 'chutes. Or, are you the type who needs to control others? If so, can you be solely responsible for how they live? Can you take responsibility for pulling their cord? At first, this kind of control might seem attractive, but it soon becomes burdensome; it soon controls you.

Each of us has a twofold responsibility, to ourselves and to others. The first is to learn to pack our own 'chute as soon as possible--to grow in caring for ourselves, knowing that we are worthwhile. The second, is to interact with others to encourage them to pack their own 'chutes. This can be done through helping others to feel good about themselves, as well as, by our personal example of how exciting and fulfilling it can be to be in charge of oneself.

It is one thing to pack your own 'chute, quite another to trust your skill and have the willingness to put it to the test. I invite you to begin today to look at what is in your 'chute and how you have it packed. Do you like what you see? Do you want to change some of it? Is it tangled with concepts that no longer make sense? Or does it need to be shaken out and to be repacked?

To relate this to your skills as a counselor--have you tried anything new lately? Are you a "by the book" type of counselor or have you allowed your own personality to become part of your counseling? Are you packing your own "counseling theory 'chute" or are you still tied to a specific technique?

Counseling . . . And time.

As I look at myself as a counselor, I can say with affirmation that I am a better counselor today than I was when I first started out. I have more confidence, I have more experience and, if you will, I have "on the job" training. I believe it is important for me to appreciate what the passage of time will do for me as a person and as a counselor.

The analogy which addresses the issue of time helps to remind us of the value of time, not only in our personal growth, but in our function as a counselor. Only with the passage of time will we be able to appreciate what has transpired in the counseling relationship. I know that many times I am not sure what the outcomes mean to the students. I have been fortunate to be in a position where, after a period of time--sometimes years--I have received a note from a student thanking me for the work we had done together. Unlike teaching, where tests are given and the teacher can get feedback on what is happening, counselors may never know the impact they have on another's life. Indeed, I believe that sometimes the student needs some distance before she can truly appreciate the total impact of the counseling experience.

Some years ago, Julie Andrews wrote a song that she used as her television show's theme song called "Time is My Friend." This concept produced some interesting thoughts for me. Rather than seeing time as a friend, many people tend to view time as THE ENEMY: "I don't have time" "Time is running out" "Stay young." One could cite many examples. So the idea of "time is a friend" could be a new one for many, one worth thinking about.

What are some of the ways time is a friend of the counselor? Time gives me the opportunity to reflect on the interaction with my students. It gives me the opportunity to step back, take a second (or third) look, and keep things in perspective. Through time I, as well as my student, can see growth--or lack of it--and that is also important.

I can help my students move through the developmental process through my constructive use of time. In some instances , the passage of time alone "solves" their problems.

Another way in which time is my friend is that with the passage of time I have been able to see my own growth. Who I am today, as a counselor, is quite different in many ways from who I was as a counselor when I first started out. Time has allowed me the opportunity to have those experiences which have made me more confident--both as a person and as a counselor. As I have become more confident, I have become a more competent counselor, teacher and, indeed, person.

It seems to me that as adults we have a responsibility to show young people that growing older "ain't all that bad." I don't know about you, but I don't care to go back to those so-called carefree adolescent years when I was all hung up on how people reacted to me. One of the more valuable ways that time is my friend is that I have become more inner-directed.

A few years ago I was working with a student who was a college senior. I don't recall the presenting problem, but in the course of one conversation it became apparent that one of the things bothering her was that she was soon to have her 21st birthday. As we talked about this, she made the comment, "I don't want to grow up!" When we explored what "growing up" meant to her, she painted a very depressing picture. I discovered that much of her concept came from the popular culture and that everyone had to look young, act young or they were nothing. I checked around and found that this young lady was not the only person who felt that growing up was bad.

I believe that those who are "grown up" have really copped-out on the younger generations by reinforcing the idea that old is bad and time is the enemy.

Of course, time alone will not provide insight or growth. Something else must happen along with the passage of time. I can recall when I was teaching in the public schools, some teachers "taught one year twenty times" and others had taught 20 years--and there is a difference.

For several years we have lived in a culture which reinforces "instant everything." Life issues get solved on TV in 30 minutes. Have a problem? Take a pill. In the class I am currently teaching, I find it difficult to get the students to set aside as little as 15 minutes a day for relaxation exercise. Those who do, find the exercise very helpful, but they seem to be in the minority. Looking at time, I have had to develop patience. Not everything happens on time. Waiting for a big event-- waiting while I "solve" my problems--so I can go on enjoying today--I know I have tomorrow.

A recent activity I have taken up is the practice of Tai Chi. It is good for my body and even better for my mind. When I do my Tai Chi I empty my mind. We need to encourage our students (and ourselves) to find that stress-free activity which will enable them to say, "Time is my friend."

Counseling and . . . Keys.

In my training as a counselor I was fortunate to be exposed to many different theories and practices. After I started working, I had many opportunities to attend workshops on and about counseling, as well as do extensive reading about counseling.

As a beginning counselor I tended to follow the training that I had received in the academic setting. I soon found out that while this training provided a good foundation, there were a number of situations I encountered that just didn't seem to fit the training. And therein lies the problem. The students **are not supposed** to fit the counselor's training. Rather the counselor needs to work with the student as a person, not as a textbook case. When I finally figured that out, I began to focus more on the student and function in ways that were consistent with my life philosophy, relating to the student as a person. The analogy of keys addresses this issue of counselor growth.

Last winter, a neighbor thought the lock on her car door was frozen. A friend helped out. He oiled the lock, but the key she gave him wouldn't go in at all. Her other car key went in but would not turn. She insisted that the first key was the right one. Suddenly, she realized she had the wrong car.

As counselors-in-training, we acquire many keys to use in our work with people. In fact, we usually graduate with a whole ring of keys and, as we work and learn, we keep adding keys to our ring. I don't know how it is for you, but for me some keys just seemed to work better. I am just more comfortable with them. Early on I had to learn not to use the same key all the time even though it was my favorite. When I fell into this trap of using the same key all the time, I ended up not unlike the person in the story above. I was sure I had the right key. Turned out, I had the wrong car!

I wonder how many times this happens to us. When we've worked in the same setting for a while, the stories begin to sound familiar. There is a temptation to think we know where the story is going and without too much thought, take a key off our ring and try to make it work. I think what can help us avoid this pitfall, is to stay new in our work and in our life.

A very important part of being a good counselor is taking care of yourself. This goes beyond your physical health and relates to your emotional health. I used to say that counseling was when you have two people in the same room talking to each other and, hopefully, the counselor was the healthier of the two. We tell others all the time to take some time to relax, to nurture their souls. What are you doing to take care of yourself? How do you keep yourself fresh and excited about counseling? Do you have your own routine of nurturing behavior? If there are others in your life, what do you do to keep those relationships exciting? Do you use the same key all the time in your own life?

I'm of the old school that says that we need to be good role models for our students. Becoming a role model is something we can't avoid even if we wanted to, so why not be the best we can be?

Counseling is like . . . The art of Tai Chi.

I believe that if we are going to be helpful counselors, we need to pay attention to our own personal growth--both as a person and as a counselor. Involved in this process is a regular review of what we have done before, how we felt about it and how we may wish to change in the future. There is something to be said for the comfort of knowing a routine, of having a certain way of behaving. We need to be comfortable enough with what we are doing so that we don't focus on the process. Yet we need to have enough awareness to keep our process dynamic. I think that the analogy of how to learn Tai Chi has much to offer us about how to learn to be a counselor.

I have been practicing Tai Chi since 1992. One time there was a period of about a month, when I was not able to practice. When I started Tai Chi again, I realized that I could pretty much pick it up where I left off. That started me thinking about my counseling skills --could I pick them up as easily? That line of thinking got me looking at the relationship about learning Tai Chi and learning how to be a counselor.

With the art of Tai Chi, the first thing I did was learn the form in small increments, each lesson adding on to what was learned before. My movements were mechanical and it was only after I practiced several weeks, that the movement became more fluid. My teacher was my role model and I worked to emulate his form and techniques. Then came that moment when he said that I was now in a position to be an instructor. Being an instructor is not being a Master. Time will probably run out on me before I can become a master. This does not mean I should be discouraged and quit. Rather, it means I should continue to practice and teach others and become as good as I can be. The more I practice, the better I become, the better role model I can be.

In the art of counseling, we all learned the form. It really doesn't matter which counseling theory we embrace, each has a technique to learn. Remember back when you were first learning? How awkward you felt? How mechanical? With a good mentor and lots of practice, the techniques became yours and you felt more comfortable with what you were doing. As in Tai Chi, the more you practice, the better you become, the better role model you can be.

Some questions come to mind--maybe you can answer them for yourself.

- Are you the same type of counselor as when you started?
- How have you changed?
- How do you feel about where you are now?
- What takes you beyond where you started?
- Do you think you are a "master" or is this something you are always striving for?
- Have you reached a plateau?
- What are you going to do about it?
- Is the movement always forward or can you slip back?
- When was the last time you paused in your

work to see if you were doing what you really wanted to do and in the way you wanted to do it.

I hope that reading these questions makes you pause and reflect. In so doing, I believe that if you really search, you will become a better counselor from the experience.

Counseling is like . . .Trusting yourself.

I have the utmost respect for the students who come see me. I want to be the best counselor possible for them as they seek out my help. In my experience I have had students who will challenge me (which is exciting) and, as a result of that, sometimes I doubt myself. When this happens I need to review my behavior to see if it is consistent with my philosophy. Most of the time it is. On those occasions when it isn't, I need to regroup and change. I have learned that many times when the student challenges me, it is because I am not behaving the way the student wants me to behave. When I am congruent with what I believe, I need to trust myself. I also need to be aware that when I doubt myself as a counselor, it is usually because of something that is going on in my life that has nothing to do with the student before me.

I've had a computer for several years and basically use it as a word processor. This past fall I decided it was time to explore other uses. To help me in this I signed up for a short course in Windows 95, even though I don't use that program at home. In the class we were encouraged to always use the same computer for our homework assignments as we used in the class.

When I would start to work on my assignments, I would become very frustrated, since I couldn't seem to do them.   One day when I was working, the instructor was there and aware of my frustration. He came over to help me and discovered that the person who had used it before me had done something to the computer which didn't allow me to do what I wanted.

Another example of not trusting myself. I use my home computer for   email (rossm@marietta.edu).   From time to time I try to get on-line and am not successful. After a time of frustration, I quit, only to go back later and get on without any problem.

A third example. There have been times when I try to print something and it won't print. I get a message that says check to make sure the printer is on, etc.   I check and the printer is on and the connections are tight. I am aware that I sometimes become impatient while waiting.

What do these three examples have to do with counseling? In the first two instances, my first reaction to not being able to do what I wanted was that there must be something I am doing wrong! It was only after I became more experienced that I figured out that sometimes it didn't matter what I did. For reasons beyond my control, I was not able to complete the task.

My first reaction was that I had done something wrong (not checking to see if the computer was set correctly for my project) which was directly related to my inexperience on the computer.

In the second example, whatever the problem was it was beyond my control.

In the third example involving impatience, I wonder if I sometimes signaled my impatience to the student? By nonverbal behavior did I indicate that I wanted them to hurry up? I have learned to walk away from the computer and when I return , it usually works. In counseling, there is also a time to move away from an issue. There is a time for things to happen and I need patience to wait for that time.

I wonder how many times as a beginning

counselor when something doesn't work out, we assume that the blame lies with us? Or do we become impatient when things don't move along the way we want them to. I'm sure I felt that way when I first started. With experience, I have learned that counseling is a collaboration between student and counselor. In teaching counseling, and in my practice, one thing I try to be aware of is who is doing the most of the work. If I am working harder than my student, then there is something wrong with the picture. I needed to learn to "trust the process." Once I let that come into my awareness, I believe I became a much better counselor.

I would suggest that this might be helpful to reflect on at the end of the day.

Counseling is like . . . A maze.

Counseling is a process and, as such, it becomes a partnership between the student and the counselor. As a process, both parties need to be involved. The counselor's role is to be sensitive to where the student is going, to allow the student to have freedom to explore, and to set the direction the counseling session will take. Because I may have made this trip before with another student, I need to remind myself that it is not the same trip because it is not the same student.

Counseling and the counseling process are somewhat difficult to explain to the uninitiated. Many times when asked "What happens in counseling?" I have found myself at a loss for an explanation. Finally, I hit upon the idea of using the analogy of a maze.

The counselor and the student enter the maze together. Depending upon the sensitivity of the counselor, and the openness of the student, progress through the first stages may take ten minutes or several counseling sessions. It is during this phase that the student "sizes up" the counselor and decides whether or not this is the person with whom to share the problems.

As the student starts through the maze, the ability of the counselor is challenged. Is the counselor able to move with the student? Is the counselor able to allow the student to set the direction? The pace? How sensitive is the counselor to where the student is? The relationship, or lack of it, established at this point may determine whether or not the relationship continues.

Let us assume that some sort of a beginning is made. What happens now? As the counselor and student move through the maze together, the sensitivity of the counselor is most important--can the counselor be aware of where the student is? Are they together or has the student left the counselor behind? Or conversely, has the counselor left the student behind? I believe that a major role of the counselor is to encourage and be supportive as the student explores the various paths or alternatives that are open. Unless the student is free to explore the alternatives moving through the maze, choosing paths and directions, the student will not learn to make decisions. At the same time, the counselor has the role of pointing out possible consequences of the various choices and helping the student to see a dead end in the maze as an alternative to reject. The counselor can also teach the student that making a poor choice does not have to translate into failure. As the two of you move through the maze there will be times when the student does not move as fast as the counselor would like or make the choices the counselor would have made. What then? The counselor needs to remember that the student acts from personal experience, and is not always likely to make the same choices the counselor would. It is important for the counselor to look at the maze through the student's eyes as well as through the "counselor detached viewpoint" and to cultivate patience.

Pacing through the maze will vary. Some sections may seem easier than others. Sometimes the student may lack confidence and need more encouragement to move forward. Sometimes the student may need to be reminded to move slower.

The counselor must always examine the reasons behind the counselor's own anxiousness about the rate of progress. Is the reason a self-serving one or a concern for the best interests of the student?

The ideal result of the counseling relationship is more than "solving" a problem. The student learns a new way of behaving--of living--so that in future problems the student is able to apply what has been learned from working through the maze. The student then will be better able to work out future problems independently.

As the counselor and the student work through the maze, the counselor continually needs to be aware of where the student is. I believe that the counselor's role is one of encouragement and support rather than that of leader through the maze. The counselor needs to keep in mind whose needs are being met, the counselor's or the student's.

CHAPTER 5

STUDENT GROWTH

I believe that the ultimate purpose of counseling is to help the students grow to their fullest potential, to enjoy a reasonably satisfying life, and to engage with others in ways that are nurturing. The analogies which follow relate to this purpose.

Counseling is like . . . Glassmaking.

Many times students' self esteem is a reflection of their academic record. I remember working with a person who was an excellent student. For her to receive less than a perfect grade was almost devastating. Her friends resented her attitude in that she would come back from taking a test and was sure she had failed. She would go on and on about it, only to find out later that she received an "A." On the other hand, her friends really struggled and were pleased to get a "C" or "B" grade on a test. This wa a source of conflict in their relationships and so, with their prodding, she ended up in my office.

When we began to explore what was going on, it became apparent that from her point of view, her self worth was dependent on doing very well in school. Somehow she had gotten the idea that no one would like her if she didn't excel in everything she did and that she would meet with her parents disapproval.

Another scene: When I was teaching in the public schools I met a young man who was not a strong academic student. On the other hand, his sister was an excellent student. The young man's self esteem was very low because of this. When I talked with him, it was apparent to me that while he was not a good student, he had many other attributes which were outstanding. This was a young man who grew up in a rural area of Michigan and who spent a lot of time in the out-of-doors. He was an excellent trapper and hunter, and had the ability to survive in the woods. When I pointed this out to him and helped him to see that there was more to life than "getting good grades," he was able to appreciate the abilities he did have.

I believe that the analogy of glassmaking would be helpful in the above situations, in that it could help students appreciate their abilities, and understand that it isn't necessary to be perfect in everything to be a good person.

Due to an abundance of natural resources, the area in which I live has several glassmaking businesses. The three I know best are: an art glass factory which makes decorative glass; a small operation that makes Victorian glass globes; and an individual artist who makes art objects.

In the art glass factory, there are several assembly lines that make a variety of items. Each assembly line makes one specific item for four hours and then the mold is changed. In the process of making the item, a specific amount of molten glass is gathered from the glory hole and then the master glass blower blows into a tube to get the glass started. Depending on the item being made, it is either swung and/or put in a mold and shaped. Next, it is heated once more and then taken to another artisan who, in the case of a vase or bowl, crimps the glass and adds an edge to it. During this process it might be returned to the glory hole several times to be reheated for remolding. When this process is done, the glass is put on a conveyer belt and moved through a cooling process. At the end of this process, there are inspectors waiting and they will do one of three things: 1) accept the piece as perfect and send it on to the next stage; 2) put it aside to be sold as a "second" in the factory retail shop; or, 3) break it and throw it in the scrap heap. However, the scrap heap is not waste. This rejected, broken glass is sold to a marble manufacturer, so it is recycled into another use. The goal of the art glass factory is to have each piece as perfect as possible, each resembling the other.

The second process, blowing glass globes, is a two person per shift operation. Again, glass is gathered from the glory hole, the tube is blown into to get a bubble started and then compressed air is used to expand it to a specific size. Next, the master craftsman swings the glass to enlarge it and shape it. Once again, the purpose is to produce globes that are exactly the right size and shape. Anything less than perfect is rejected.

The third process, that of the individual artist, also starts out by gathering the glass from the glory hole. But then the process changes. The artist begins to gather bits of colored glass on the hot glass. He may do this several times to build the glass into an orb. The goal, in this process, is to have the orbs all the same size, but different in style.

So how does one relate this to counseling? I have the feeling that sometimes students think that only perfection is acceptable and that everyone should be alike.

This message is given to them in so many ways, but primarily by grades. Only all "A's" are good, anything less is not acceptable. And they must be good in all subjects. If they dare to be different it is not quite right. Maybe we need to make room for those who are very good, but not perfect.

How about the person who is not good in one area, but excels in another? A student I worked with several years ago came from a family of doctors. He, too was to become a doctor.   However, he disliked science and didn't want to major in it.   His solution was to flunk out of school.   A year later he came back as an English major, graduated and attended graduate school where he earned a Ph. D. in English. The last I heard he was very happy teaching English in a major university.

My friend who makes orbs doesn't know what they are going to look like when he starts out.   What he does know is when he puts together beautiful pieces of glass , the orb will be beautiful.   Can we do this with students? Encourage them to experiment, find the place that seems good to them, explore what that means and believe that the final outcome will be beautiful. I believe that is what counseling is all about. We need to encourage people to find what is right for them. It is all right to not be like everyone else and to have the courage to try being themselves.

Counseling is like . . Planning a trip.

Some students are reluctant to see a counselor because of a fear that they will lose control over their lives. Many of them have grown up in an environment where others want to tell them how to live. Even though this is done with the best of intentions, it just isn't effective. They can't know what the other is looking for in life. While some students may believe they want others to tell them what to do, they really don't. One of the advantages of having others tell you how to live, is that if it doesn't work out, you can blame someone else for your failures. All of us need to be responsible for ourselves because no one else can be.

Part of growing is learning the value of making our own decisions. I use the analogy of planning a trip as a way of helping students understand this.

I had the opportunity to take a trip one summer and as I talked about it before I left, a common question was, "Are you going with a group?" My response was "No." I didn't want to take someone else's trip. I had decided what

I wanted to do, where I wanted to go, and how much time I wanted to spend there. Having made my initial plans, I turned them over to a travel agent to make reservations for me. When this had been done, I made the necessary changes so the trip reflected what I wanted to do, where I wanted to go, and the time schedule I wanted to keep.

Counseling is a lot like this. We can help students explore what they think they want to do and make suggestions based on our own experiences. We can be the "travel agent" in helping them negotiate some of the hurdles but, in the end, they are the ones who take the trip. While the trip they take might not be the one we would wish for them, nevertheless, they are the ones who will do the traveling. We need to respect that. One of the things I am becoming more aware of as I work with young people is, they don't have the same timetable I had at their age. They seem to be much more willing to take a longer time for their trip through college. Without putting a value judgment on that, I do need to have that awareness.

As with my own travel agent, I wanted and needed to draw on their experience. I also wanted the opportunity to make changes that made sense to me. We need to give this same freedom to our students. Because I was an integral part of planning my trip, it reflected my wants and needs. Therefore, it was more enjoyable. So it is with our students. When they are a part of the planning process, their "trip" will be much more enjoyable and meaningful.

I needed and depended upon my travel agent for important information. Our students will also need and depend upon us for important information. Together we can plan a trip that they will take and grow from. Perhaps most importantly, it is in this process that we empower them to take charge of their own lives.

Counseling is like . . . Duplicate bridge.

Many times, when students come into counseling, they feel overwhelmed by their past and believe that they have no impact on what the future may hold for them. They also believe they are stuck with what has gone on before. When I sense this is an issue for the student, I use the analogy of duplicate bridge. This will help them to understand that no matter what their past may be, they are not stuck there. With help and support, they will be able to " play their cards" in new ways to change what the outcome can be.

Their histories will help them to understand where they are now, how they got there, but it does not freeze them in a particular style of living. Students can become more than who they were in the past. Each person has choices to make, and the choices are not always easy. They need to be on guard to be sure that they don't fall back into old unhealthy ways. Students can learn from the past and, through counseling, can change their course in life.

I don't play duplicate bridge, but I am told by a friend of mine who does, that it works something like this. A foursome sits down at a table where the cards have already been dealt. As they play the cards, they keep the cards in front of them so that the hands remain intact. When they have finished playing the hand, they leave each hand in place and another foursome comes along and plays the same cards. The object of the game is not so much to win, but rather to play the hands the best way you can. In this situation, there are some preset conditions and the players must do the best job possible under the conditions that have already been established.

I see a parallel between duplicate bridge and counseling. When a student comes to see me, the student brings with him the accumulation of all that has happened up to that moment. Neither the counselor nor the student can control what has gone on in the past. However, we both must be cognizant of what history the student brings. More and more I am becoming aware of the concept that I do family counseling minus some of the family members. Who the student is in front of me has been greatly affected by the student's history.

In working with the student, my focus is more likely to be "how can you help yourself?" "What can you do to make things better for yourself?" When we do talk about history, it is in terms of how it is affecting the student right now. [It is easy to place blame and allow ourselves to get caught up in the game of helplessness.] I work to be very clear with the student that when we do look at the student's history, it is not to find fault or blame. Rather, the focus is on understanding what has happened to bring the student to this time and place. As a youngest child, I am well aware that each family member has a unique reaction to a situation. As a counselor, I must have that awareness about my client.

I see my role as helping the students learn how to "play the cards they have been dealt" in the best possible way. We need to explore all the options. This way students can begin to reclaim the power (control) over their life and realize that even though the "cards have been dealt," it is the student who must choose how to play the cards.

Virginia Satir alludes to this in *Peoplemaking,* when she says to take three or four objects and find at least three different ways to balance them. The point being that there is more than one option in any situation. The important thing is to search for the options and not to settle for the first one you discover (Satir. p. 120)

Our job as counselors is to help students explore their options, to examine them before jumping at the first one that comes to mind.

Counseling is like . . . A circuit breaker box.

On occasion I have students arrive in my office with a sense that their world is falling apart. Some small event has caused them to panic and they don't understand why this is so. Something they usually can handle without any problem at all has suddenly thrown them into a panic. As we explore this, it becomes apparent that they are on overload, that several small events have led up to their present state. Because the events were small, the students didn't deal with them and they piled up. To help them understand what is happening to them, I use the analogy of the circuit breaker box.

The box is built to handle a specific amount of energy. If you overload the circuit, the breaker will go off and not work. [The circuit is broken.] Therefore, you have no power to provide for those demands it usually serves.

Depending on the amount of overload and the cause for the broken circuit, you may be able to fix it yourself. That is, if the cause of the problem is a slight overload, you are able to deal with this by resetting the broken circuit. However, if there is a major cause for the broken circuit, it is necessary to call in someone with a considerable amount of expertise to investigate the cause and deal with it . For you to reset the circuit solves the problem for a short period. However, if the circuit is broken again and again, it can amplify the problem to the point where it would result in total destruction, i.e., a fire. The severity of the problem determines the degree of expertise required to handle it.

Applying this to counseling, the student has the source of energy (confidence, self worth, esteem) to be able to handle some things. If the student has no reserve as a result of past failure, when a problem arises the student "blows a circuit." If the student has a minimal reserve (or none) the job of the counselor is to help the student build this reserve.

With people, this reserve power comes from growing. As the student grows, reserve power is generated which the person can use when needed. If the student is not encouraged to grow, in this case through dealing with problems, a reserve is never built. I see the function of the counselor as helping the student assess how much reserve is available so that the student is not asked to handle something for which there is not enough strength, resulting in a circuit being blown. At the same time, it is important to allow (encourage) the student to handle the things the student is ready to handle and thereby gain reserve power through growth. The counselor needs to develop that degree of sensitivity which allows the counselor to facilitate the student's exploration of strength. The student will then begin to know the amount of strength available.

The counselor also needs to have the inner strength (guts?) to allow the student to experience the minimal risk of throwing one switch, but not the whole circuit. If the counselor protects the student from taking this risk, the counselor gets in the way of the student's growth. The counselor needs to strike a balance which will allow the student to assume responsibility to the degree to which the student is able to do so successfully and thereby increase self worth. Hopefully the end result is student growth to the extent that the student is able to be in charge of the "power plant."

Counseling is like . . Jell-O looking for a mold.

When students come to college they have an identity based on their high school experience. They may be (say) at the top of their class, or the star athlete, or the most popular student in their class. In college they encounter others who have had that same identity in high school, and in some cases, others are even better than they were. This is a very difficult adjustment to make. I have often thought that freshmen men had the most difficult time of all students. They truly are "low man" on the list. Freshmen women often prefer dating upper-class men. The freshmen men find themselves struggling to establish themselves in sports where once they were already stars. When you find that others in your college class were at the top of their high school class, and their senior class is larger than your whole high school, it is easy to become overwhelmed.

Using the analogy of Jell-O looking for a mold helps these young people to understand what is going on in their world. It illustrates that in time, they will find their place of belonging. It may look different than their place in high school, and maybe that's good, and it will be a belonging place for them

While thinking about college freshmen and some of the issues they will encounter at college, I came up with the analogy that freshmen are like "Jell-O looking for a mold." As high school students, each has an identity which has been shaped over the years--scholar, athlete, air head, class clown, nerd, etc. That is their mold, even though the Jell-O hasn't firmed up yet. When the students are "turned out," e.g., graduated from high school, they retain the shape, but it is seldom solid. Upon coming to college, meeting new people and new environments, freshmen begin to lose their old identity. For example, the high school star is in competition with many "stars." The student who was well known in high school is reduced to being one of many unknowns. The "most likely to succeed" is one of many in that category.

As a result, a lot of time is spent during the first semester looking for a new mold, something familiar, something which will fit the old shape. Even though that "old shape" may not be the best one to have, at least it is known. Their boundaries (molds) are not clear and sometimes an individual student is not quite sure "who is me" and "who is not me." As a result of this looking, one of the things I have observed is that it is quite easy for freshmen to become enmeshed with each other. For example, confusion about which are "my problems" and which belong to "my roommate."

Many freshmen encounter freedoms they have never had before. The freedom to sleep all day and stay up all night; the freedom to go to class or not go to class. This is a time of much experimentation, a time to push the limits. Some have the maturity to handle this responsibility and some get into trouble. All of this is a vital part of the search for the mold.

For many students, the mold may be their choice of a major. For some the mold quickly drops away when after a week of classes they decide that the major they thought was right for them, is not what they want. For some, the mold may be their athletic ability. If they get cut from the team or an injury makes it impossible to play, they lose their mold. For others, it is their academic achievement and the first test on which they receive a "C" breaks their mold. As you might suspect, all of these affect their self esteem. They are at a loss as to what to do to make themselves feel better, since all the things they used to do for self esteem, no longer work.

Part of my job, and the role of the college, is to help students understand that this searching is a part of growing. As painful as it is at times, it is nevertheless a part of being 18 years old, or older, and a college freshman.

Some students may find a mold that feels good and fits during their first year of college. Other students may need two, three or four years to find that mold which seems right for them. One of the things we need to help our students understand is that, throughout their lifetime, there will be many molds which can be an exciting part of living. If the students can accept the search as a part of the process of growing, it will be less traumatic. Indeed, there are dangers of finding molds too soon because, for the most part, students don't have all the information they need to make the best decision. Freshmen need to be careful not to grab the first mold that comes along and force it to fit. That might be comforting for a while, but if it isn't the right mold for them, it will become very uncomfortable in a short time.

Counseling is like . . . Forsythia.

Because of our experience, sometimes there is a temptation to "push" students in certain directions, which we know are good for them. After all, look at all the experience we have had! Sometimes students will want us to tell them what to do and they will just do it. I use the analogy of forsythia to remind both of us of the importance of allowing growth to take the time necessary for solid growth. Yes, we can push the student along on our time schedule, but we need to ask ourselves if that is really in the best interest of the student. I don't know the meaning of "grow up." This suggests to me that at some magical time we are all grown up and that's it! My own belief is that growing is an ongoing process over time and hopefully, never ends. Regardless of age or experience, there is always one more thing to learn.

A fairly common practice at the end of February or in March is to cut off a few shoots of a forsythia bush and bring them inside, place them in water and wait for them to blossom. Of course, they will have a more limited life since the shoots are cut off from their roots.

If you wait for the shrub to blossom outside, it will take longer, depending on many conditions, such as weather and temperature. However, these blossoms will last longer because the branches are connected to roots and get nurturing from the soil.

Counseling is sometimes like this. It is possible for the counselor to attempt to force growth and may even appear to succeed. However, if this growth is on the counselor's time schedule and not the student's, the results will be limited since the student is not firmly "grounded." That is, the changes have been forced before the student is ready.

On the other hand, when the counselor nurtures and supports the student by allowing the student to set the pace, the results are usually more solid since the student has not been cut off from the roots of their value system. There is a strong foundation to support and nurture the growth.

I find that the people I work with know

their time schedules much better than I. It is important for me to respect the student's time schedule and not allow my needs to get in the way of the student blossoming.

CHAPTER 6

HABITS AND GOOD MENTAL HEALTH

Good mental health is more than the absence of mental illness. Good mental health implies that individuals are capable of interacting with others in such a way as to enhance their own growth, as well as the growth of others. The analogies that follow relate to the issues of good mental health and make some suggestions as to what we can do to maintain good mental health.

Counseling is like . . .Keeping good habits.

One thing I know about myself, and I suspect is true of others, is that I have a lot of knowledge about what is good for me-- mentally and physically. The gap seems to come in putting that knowledge into practice. An observation I have made over the years is that after the 1st of a new year, my local YMCA is filled with people who have made those New Year's resolutions. It is almost impossible to find a place to park. After about three weeks, parking is much easier. People start out with the best of intentions, but somewhere the motivation drops off. On the other hand, I have no trouble at all keeping my unhealthy habits! As a way of understanding this, I use the analogy of buckling up my seat belt. It suggests that the key to keeping good habits is an attitude. It also helps to have a support system, someone who will check in with us on how we are doing.

One of the ways I motivate myself to get up and swim every morning, is that I don't give myself a choice. This is what I do. The decision is made and that helps me to stay on track--at least with swimming. There is also a subtle peer pressure. People are used to seeing me everyday and if I don't show up, the next time I do, I'm asked if I have been ill.

For several years now, the first thing I do when I get into my car is to fasten my seat belt. This has become such an automatic habit that when I get in the car just to back it out of the garage, I fasten my seal belt. Then, one day it happened! My seat belt buckle broke. I felt naked! I immediately went to the dealer to see it if could be fixed and, if not, order a new one. As I write this, I have now been without my seal belt for one week. For the first few times I got in the car, I reached for my seat belt, but now I have discovered that I no longer miss it. This seems to make a pretty strong statement about habits. I can safely make that a stronger statement--it says something about good habits. As I sit writing this, I'm thinking about the struggle I've had breaking poor eating habits. I grew up in a family and at an age where the worst thing you could do was not clean up your plate. In my case, this has led to putting on weight. As I have become more sensitive to my body and what I do to it, I have been working at losing weight. And it is WORK. Breaking old eating habits, which are not good, have proven to be quite difficult. But, as I indicated above, I am amazed at how easy it is to get out of the good habit of reaching for my seat belt. So my statement comes down to how easy it is to not do those things which we know are good for us.

Since I like to think in terms of analogies, I tried to relate this to living and good mental health. The way it makes the most sense to me is that I know what is good for me. I know what makes me feel good. I know the kinds of things I should or should not do to promote my own mental health. And sometimes I neglect to practice those growth producing habits. It doesn't take long for me to get on a downward spiral and if I don't catch myself, the first thing I know is that I've gotten caught up in self defeating behaviors. I don't "buckle my seat belt" or practice good mental health habits. I don't do those things which help me feel good.

How about you? Do you "buckle your mental health seat belts?" Do you take the effort and exercise the control you have over your own life to do those things which you know have a positive affect on your own mental health? As I wrote that last sentence, I was reminded of the book by Glasser, (1985) *Positive Addiction*, in which he talks about the need to become addicted to those practices and activities which have a positive outcome for our mental health. What we need to do is practice good mental health activities to the point where we become uncomfortable when we forget to do them.

As I talk with friends who are in the helping profession, one thing seems to come out very often. We are pretty good at helping others develop good mental health practices but all too often we forget to relate what we know to our own lives. Whatever the reasons, and we are usually pretty good at rationalizing, we leave our own seat belts unfastened. I would argue that the most important thing we have to "give" to our students is our personal practice of growth producing mental health activities. Obviously, what these practices are might be different for each of us. We must know ourselves and search within to find out what is appropriate.

Counseling is like . . . Chaos.

Oftentimes students arrive in my office in a state of panic. When we are able to figure out what is going on, it often deals with something they are doing that is not working for them as it had in the past. This throws them into a state of chaos. Once they have calmed down, I work to help them see that rather than panic at the situation, this is an opportunity for them to evaluate and sort out new ways of being. I use the analogy of chaos to help the students understand that rather than the "end of the world," this is an opportunity for growth.

In a recent issue of a newsletter I receive, there was an article by Richard H. Lee, P. E., on the topic of therapeutic chaos. The article was referring to the human body and the importance of learning how to relax muscle tension and other physical aspects.

One of the premises Lee suggests is that chaos is opportunity. The opportunity to restructure how we walk, breath, etc. which can have an impact on our physical health. This started me thinking about the opportunity chaos can offer in the area of mental health. One of my favorite definitions of mental illness is when a person keeps doing the same thing over and over with the hope of a different outcome. While I didn't consider most of my students to be mentally ill, many followed the definition of doing the same behavior over and over again, with the expectation of a different outcome.

In working with students, I was painfully aware of how difficult it was to get them to do something different. They would hang on to the old behaviors out of fear of the unknown, or out of an unwillingness to believe that doing something different could be helpful. It seemed so important to hang on to the familiar, no matter how ineffective it could be in either personal relationships or in academic affairs.

For some of the students the shock of being put on academic probation served to provide the chaos which helped them to look at new ways of doing academic work. Some could adapt right away, while others still clung to their old beliefs. The approach was "if I just study more it will help," ignoring the fact that they were using the wrong study techniques.

I also encountered this phenomena in the realm of personal relationships. Many seemed unwilling or unable to grasp the concept that whatever they were doing wasn't working.

It seems to me that one of the jobs of the counselor is to help students learn how to manage the chaos in their life, so that change can take place. I used to tell some students that things could get worse before they get better and I needed a commitment from them that they would work with me through this chaos. Breaking down old ineffective behaviors is hard work. And, it is scary. The unknown always is. If we can help students see the opportunity to restructure their beliefs and habits into a more flexible approach, then they will be better able to cope with life experiences. For some students, this will be a long and involved process. How long the process is will depend on their support system. Many young people don't want others to change and peer pressure can be very powerful. This is where the counselor must provide a strong support system and perhaps help the student move beyond the current peer group into a group that is more healthy for the student.

Counseling is like . . . Being stuck in the snow.

On a number of occasions I have encountered students who are having difficulty in a situation and believe that the way to succeed is to keep doing what they are doing over and over again. In the realm of academic success, I have seen students spending more time using the same approach to studying, when what they need to do, is to learn a new approach. This also happens in the realm of personal relationships. Rather than looking at their behavior and discovering that they need to change, they keep repeating the same behavior that is not successful for them. It is sometimes difficult to get them to back off and take a good look at what they are doing and how it is not working for them. What they need to do is reevaluate their situation and look for new ways to approach, solve or deal with their issues.

A way I have of getting students to explore changing is to use the analogy of being stuck in the snow. Here they see the impact of what they have been doing, how they have been stuck, and the need to change. When they have reached this point we are then able to explore different ways of behaving.

The other day I was working with someone and he made the comment, "I seem to be stuck. I have been doing the same thing over and over and can't seem to get anywhere!"

My comment to him was, "Stop what you are doing!" I went on to explain by the use of an analogy.

Since this young man was from the northeast, I asked him if he had ever been stuck in the snow. When he said yes, I asked him what he did to get out. His reply was he got out of the car and either shoveled snow or pushed the car. This usually resulted in getting unstuck. I pointed out to him that before he could get out of the car and push, he first had to stop what he was doing. If he had continued to push the accelerator, he would only get in deeper and deeper. He could get in so deep it would take a tow truck to get the car out.

In using this analogy with counseling, once you get "stuck," you keep repeating the same behavior over and over. Before you can do anything else, you need to stop this behavior. Once you have stopped, it is possible to pause, take a look at what is going on, and use some other strategy to get "unstuck."

This seems so obvious, yet many times we keep repeating the old behavior over and over and get stuck. I am reminded of Glasser's *Reality Therapy* when he advises that if whatever you are doing doesn't work, Stop! Yet many of us seem to find this difficult to do.

I suggested to this young man that he needed to keep the image of "spinning wheels" in his head, and to monitor his behavior to make sure that he wasn't' digging himself in deeper.

Counseling is like. . . Riding a two wheel mental health bicycle.

Counseling is an opportunity for growth. We are all often "stuck" in old patterns of living which are no longer effective for us. Yet, even if we are aware of this, it is very difficult to change. The familiar gives us a sense of confidence even though it may be very painful. We often don't trust ourselves to know how to change. Or, what if we did change and we were worse off than before? The analogy of learning how to ride a two wheel mental health bicycle helps the students to appreciate the value of change and what might be involved in the process.

When I encounter a student in counseling, one of my goals is to provide the opportunity for change. I find that while the student has come to the office, the idea of change is somewhat scary. The known is always more comfortable than the unknown, even if the "known" is distressful. A way to help the student appreciate the need for change is to talk about it in terms of riding a bicycle. My ability to be stable on a bike and remain upright, depends on my ability to change. That is, as I ride down the street, I am always in the process of changing, shifting my weight so that I can have stability.   Most of the time, this movement is so automatic I am not even aware of it.

I became painfully aware of this phenomena when I tried to ride a three wheel bike and ran into the mailbox! A three wheel bike is very rigid and does not require the rider to make any compensation for stability. Because of my experience riding a two wheel bike, I attempted to make these changes on a three wheeler and ended up not being able to ride the bike.

I think living is a lot like this. Many times we need to make subtle adjustments as we encounter different people and situations. I would suggest that healthy people ride "two wheel mental health bikes."   In order for us to remain stable, it is necessary to make adjustments in life. Many times these adjustments are so small we are unaware of them. At other times, the changes might be very dramatic. I believe that one of the things students seek out in counseling is to learn how to cope with change and make adjustments.

There is a choice--to ride the three wheel bike and risk running into problems because we are so rigid or, ride the two wheel bike and make those many adjustments which do lead to a more healthy life.

And from *I Want To Change But I Don't Know How* . (Rusk & read).

Before
you
know
how
to
ride
a bicycle,
you
don't
know
how
t o
ride
a
bicycle.

Counseling is like . . .Being a dietitian.

Students often get frustrated with counseling because they have a belief that if they come once, and we talk about something, that should be it. They perceive that they should be able to make the necessary changes in their lives. One of my roles as a counselor is to help them appreciate that growth and new learning take time. No one can say how much time it will take, since this varies from student to student. There is a need to let go of old behaviors and then adopt new behaviors. The analogy of counseling and being a dietitian helps the students to understand the process that is necessary for growth and change.

Learning is like eating food. Food must be assimilated in our body --so too must our learning. I would suggest to you that one of the roles of the counselor is to teach our students to learn new ways of being and doing.

I am aware that most of us don't always eat in a nutritional way. We may eat a well balanced meal once in a while, but for the most part, we have too much of one of the food groups and not enough of another, or perhaps none at all. Then there is JUNK food; eating too much sugar. And drinking too much caffeine.

So too, a student may have "junk food" living habits, not taking care of the physical self and doing little or no exercise. College students are notorious for poor sleep habits-- staying up late hours, burning the candle at both ends.

These "junk food" living habits affect emotional stability. As dietitian-counselor, I see our job as helping the student to choose from each of the basic "food groups" for living. For example, these food groups could include: sleep; exercise; relaxation time; study time and social time. Choosing from each of these groups helps the student appreciate the need for a well balanced life.

As with healthy eating habits, it takes time to assimilate this learning. If you have ever tried to change eating habits, you know what I mean. We have to take the student slowly through the process so that the learning can become a part of the student's life style. The person who has never exercised for instance, can't expect to start out on a full regiment of exercise and stay with it. It is necessary to start out slowly so the student can begin to experience the changes. I once had someone say to me "I diet everyday at every meal." In other words, instead of going on a crash diet or a two week plan, he worked on it every day. We need to teach our students that good emotional health involves good physical and good mental health habits. We must work on them everyday to change our lifestyles.

When a person begins new ways of living, quite often this new plan works for a few days and the student slips. When this happens, the result is often to give up. Our job is to help the student understand that slips happen and the student can start again the next day. This is not a reason to give up.

Learning is assimilated over time through daily review. And the student must appreciate that learning new life styles takes place over time with practice. In the educational setting, we have tests to see how well we have learned. In counseling, we need to provide feedback to help our students "know" they have learned. There are many ways to do this. I suggest journal writing is a great way to check out how far we have come.

Counseling is like . . . Aladdin's lamp.
(contributed by Lucinda Pyatt)

Students often find their way to the counselor's office because of failing grades. Sometimes the student is required to work with the counselor as part of their academic probation. This can lead to resistance, a perfect time for the non-confrontational analogy.

Sometimes the student simply needs to learn some study skills. But often there is a more significant problem. How well a student does in school, or in life, is determined in large measure by his level of self-esteem. The underachiever, especially, is not reaching his potential because he does not believe he is worthy of any greater achievements.

Since most young people have either read the story of "Aladdin and the Wonderful Lamp" or have seen the Disney movie version, the following analogy can be useful.

The cornerstone of good mental health is self-esteem. And self-esteem, like an Aladdin's Lamp, offers great power to its possessor, power which can be used for good or evil, selfishly or unselfishly.

Like the lamp in the story of "Aladdin and the Wonderful Lamp," self-esteem is often a lost and hidden treasure. It must be sought out in the dark cave of our inner self. And, like the lamp, it might not be easily recognized as a treasure because it is brass rather than gold or silver, commonplace and accessible to all. How often is this lamp overlooked or undervalued? Aladdin's princess thought the lamp worthless and traded it to the magician for a new lamp. Her failure to value the lamp, because of its common appearance, caused her to lose the lamp and its power. . . a value choice that was nearly her undoing.

The power of the lamp, like a person's self-esteem, is very strong. But it is only available if summoned and commanded. The genie of the lamp could not act on his own. And the genie could only be summoned by rubbing of the lamp. Often we, like the lamp, need polishing and find that an abrasive rubbing summons a power within us that we had forgotten was there.

Acquisition of the magic lamp was accomplished in various ways in Aladdin's story. The magician sought to have the lamp through deceptions and through other people. The princess took it from her husband's bed chamber, thinking it a worthless piece of metal. Aladdin acquired it through diligence and courage. He valued it but did not worship it and never abused its power. We see people around us, hopefully not ourselves, trying to find their self worth by lying, cheating, and abusing others. We also see persons who find their self worth in their spouse or some other person. And then, of course, there are the

Aladdins who, through courage and hard work, learn to value themselves without conceit, who are self-caring without selfishness.

How do we lose our self-esteem? The magician was the first in the story to lose the lamp. He first lost it by refusing to help Aladdin out of the cave, not trusting Aladdin. Ultimately he lost it by falling asleep in the midst of his thievery. Aladdin lost the lamp by leaving it behind in the care of another when he went out on the hunt. The princess lost it by not valuing it as much as something that was newer and shinier. In every instance the lamp was lost because of shortsightedness, carelessness, or neglect. So it is with our self-esteem. If we take it for granted, undervalue its importance to our well-being, we may lose it. Then, like Aladdin, we must summon our courage and diligently work to restore it again.

Self-esteem, of course, is not magic. It will not, when summoned, bring us a splendid silver tray "set out with the choicest viands on a dozen golden platters, and flagons of wine and crystal goblets." However, with self-confidence and determination of a powerful self-esteem we can achieve far greater feats than we had ever imagined. We can make our own magic happen.

CHAPTER 7

RELATIONSHIPS

Certainly a major part of the issues dealt with in counseling, relate to relationships. There is the relationship between the counselor and the student, as well as peer relationships. Many counseling sessions revolve around peer relationships--roommates, best friends, significant others on campus, as well as, the relationships that were left behind when the student came to college. The following analogies can provide insight on some approaches to helping students with these various relationships.

Counseling is like . . . Fruit farming.

When students come to college for the first time, they leave behind many friends. In order to fill the gap, there is almost a panic to find new friends. Many have been told the myth that "your roommate will be your best friend" and so some try to force a relationship with their roommate. When this doesn't work, they often end up in my office. My first job is to dispel the myth. Roommates often are best friends, AFTER they have had an opportunity to make a choice as to who that roommate will be. That doesn't usually happen the first semester of your freshman year. When we get over that hurdle, I use the analogy of fruit farming to help them understand that friendships need to be nurtured--that you can't force them to grow. All encounters will not turn into close friendships, and that is as it should be.

The area of relationships is an issue that is faced by many college freshmen. This issue has many facets to it. For some, it involves the attempt to retain a high school relationship that has lost its commonality. For others, in their search for new relationships, they grab the first person that comes along and try to make that person "their new best friend." Both of these experiences can be very painful.

One way of thinking about human relationships is to think of a fruit farmer. First, the farmer prepares the ground, then plants the seedlings. At this point he does not sit back and wait for things to happen. Rather, he provides nurture for the seedlings by giving them food, taking care of the weeds so that the growth is not choked out. He continues this caring until the seeding has grown to maturity.

So it is with human relationships. We cannot sit back and wait for nature to take its course. Instead, it is important that we care and let others know we care. We do the things necessary to nurture the relationship, and make sure that the weeds of suspicion, jealousy, possessiveness, etc., don't take over. We must cultivate the relationship and make sure that only those things which will foster growth are allowed to be part of the relationship. Like the fruit tree, our relationships bear fruit when properly tended, cultivated, nourished, and pruned of the dead wood. When we stubbornly hang on to parts of a relationship that have died, we risk losing that relationship.

The fruit tree must have a balance of nutrients from the sun, the rain, and the soil. Relationships also thrive on a variety of common interests and concerns. Frequently, relationships wither because interests change the people involved and no new common interests have been nurtured. Eventually the relationship dies of starvation.

What causes relationships to end? Perhaps one of the major causes is that one person continues to grow while the other has reached a plateau. As with the orchard, if one row grows so that the other row is cast in the shadow, the second row will not grow as tall. Gail Sheehy, in her book *Passages*, suggests that we have different time periods of growth, and if these happen to be "out of sync." , a relationship can falter.

If a seedling is left in a pot that is too small, then its growth will be affected. It needs more room to grow. We also know that when a plant is first transplanted, this is a major trauma, requiring a lot of special care for a while. So it is with people. A relationship can die by being smothered, crowded into too small a pot or neglected after it is moved. I remember reading a quote a long time ago which says it well: "Let there be spaces in your relationship."

Relationships need room to grow, and need new things added to stimulate growth. When new things first begin to enter a relationship it is not unlike a plant that has been transplanted. In new environments relationships may falter. With loving care, most likely, the relationship will survive.

Fruit trees do not bear fruit all year long. They have a cycle of blooming, bearing fruit and resting--a process of cycling and rebirth. Often our relationships move in similar cycles. Friends move in and out of our lives. When a relationship is no longer alive, nothing can make it bloom. When one person no longer wants a relationship, the other cannot make the relationship happen. One must let go of the other, so that both may continue to grow.

Counseling is like. . .Change management.

The transition from high school to college can be painful at times. The students leave their secure, known world of high school and venture into unknown territory. What will it hold for them? For some it is a welcome change from their high school experience. For others the great unknown is frightening, even though they wouldn't admit it. In addition to a geographical change, the students are also undergoing some social change, having their values challenged, encountering others who could be quite different from who they are. Then there is the intellectual change. Instead of learning facts, many college classes challenge students to think, to conceptualize, to develop their thoughts.
I believe that one of our jobs as counselors is to help the students see this change as a wonderful opportunity to grow and learn. If we are to do that, we must be in

touch with what some of those changes are. I would offer you this analogy of change to help you reflect on what some of the changes facing our young people might be. I know they are far different from the challenges I faced as a college freshman.

In 1993, as part of the commemoration of the 500th anniversary of Columbus' trip to the Americas, Columbus, Ohio hosted the Ameriflora Exhibit. I had the opportunity to visit the Smithsonian exhibit, Seeds of Change, which was a part of the major exhibit. The "seeds of change" referred to in the exhibit were, corn, potatoes, sugar, horses and disease. These five items changed the course of history and civilization as a result of Columbus' voyage. I won't go into detail, but leave it to you to think about what the impact of these five "seeds of change" had on civilization 500 years ago, as well as, today.

This concept started me thinking about the impact of change on my life (no, it didn't take place over 500 years!) While I could list many things, I will note only one at this point, the launching of Sputnik into space by the Russians. From that came the National Defense Education Act which provided me with the opportunity to return to school for a degree in counseling, which totally changed the focus of my life.

Historians have always pointed out the impact of discoveries on who we are and how we live. I can't help but think about the many new things that have occurred in the lives of the young people with whom we work and what the impact of these new things has been. Rather than try to list all the changes that have taken place in the last 20 years, I think it might be more productive to think about what we, as counselors, can do to help young people deal with these changes. I think we can agree that the status quo is always easier to handle when we think we know what it is we are dealing with. Things might not be O. K., but we at least know what the "things" are. And we all know there is no such thing as the status quo.

As I look around and become aware of all the issues our young people have to deal with, I get overwhelmed. What must it be like for them? What can counselors do to help young people learn how to deal with these many changes? It seems to me that what we need to do is to develop a basic strategy to help them be firmly grounded in themselves and learn to like themselves.

This is no small task. It is important to help them grow in self esteem, sometimes IN SPITE OF, not because of, their background.

The days of Dick and Jane and a dog named Spot are gone, if indeed, they ever did exist. We need to help people let go of the myths so that they can better deal with the realities.

I know what I have put before you is not an easy task. You, too, are also pulled in many directions in the course of a day. However, what I ask of you does not necessarily require a major effort on your part.

Take time, right now, to reflect on one small different way of being with your students that will impact those with whom you work. It can be just one small act.

For the last three years I have taught Tai Chi to the residents of a juvenile center. I spent about a total of nine hours with them each year. Let me quote from a few of their thank you notes and let them speak for themselves. "I wanted to thank you for the Tai Chi. At first I thought it was a little strange, but then I started to like it because for the first time in many months I started to feel a sense of accomplishment."(boy) "By teaching me Tai Chi I learned to trust myself more. I learned a lot from the talks we had every Friday."(girl) "What you taught me helps me to control my anger a little better. I am very thankful to you."(boy) "I just wanted to thank you for taking your time to come here and to teach us Tai Chi. Because of Tai Chi I have learned a new and relaxing way to relieve stress."(girl)

When you let others know that you value them and that you believe they have worth, they will prove that you are right.

Counseling is like. . . Discovering the kind of gardener you are.

How long has it been since you stopped and reflected on how you are working with students? Have you changed how you interact with them in the last few years? When was the last time you went to a seminar or workshop on counseling and counseling skills? Have you experimented with what you learned? Do you interact with all students in the same way? Does this seem appropriate? When was the last time you deliberately changed the way you listened to students? Have you ever taken a day and decided to focus on just one aspect of your interaction with students?

I believe these are questions we should ask ourselves on a regular basis. To help motivate you to do this, I offer the analogy of "discovering the kind of gardener you are." You may find that you like what you see, or you may wish to take this opportunity to experiment and grow. After all, isn't that what we ask of our students?

I recently attended a seminar on empowering win-win agreements. In the seminar, the model presented was that some people view an organization with a mechanical paradigm or mindset. The organization is like a machine. If something is broken, it needs to be fixed. If you can find the problem, get the right part, stick it in, turn it on, and then it will work.

On the other hand, there are some who see the organization as an organic paradigm. That is to say, they see it as a living, growing thing made up of living, growing people. Living things are not immediately "fixed" by replacing non-working parts. They are nurtured over time to produce desired results. The presenter went on to say that the desired results are created by the gardener. The gardener knows that life is within the seed. Although it may be impossible to make the seed grow, the gardener can select the best seed and use skill and knowledge to create the best conditions, correct soil temperature, adequate sunshine, water, fertilizer, weeding, cultivation, and time, which will maximize growth.

I couldn't help but reflect on counselors I

have known. I know that there were those who saw a client as someone who was broken and it was the counselor's job to find the broken part, fix it or replace it.

I'm happy to say that the majority of counselors I have known, look at clients as growing organisms. When something was wrong, the counselor's job was to nurture the life before her. To seek, with the client, the optimum conditions in which growth could take place. The counselor-gardener also knows that you can not force the change to take place. All the counselor can do is work to make the conditions as nurturing as possible. This can take many forms. I will never forget one of my very early students. After greeting her, we sat down to begin our session. but she said nothing. Eye contact was made from time to time and I could only hope that my non-verbals suggested my willingness to listen. The student still said nothing. As you might imagine, this neophyte counselor was anxious! I could see that the student was comfortable, so I was smart enough not to say anything. After 45 minutes, I indicated to the student that the time was about up and did she want to say anything? Nothing! When the session was over, she said to me, "Thanks for letting me sit here quietly. I really needed to be in a safe place where I could just sit and think without anyone asking questions." Upon reflection, I believe I was providing conditions which could maximize growth. Thank goodness I kept my mouth shut!

Counseling is like . . . Watching a tree grow.

In June, I usually spend some time thinking back over the year, and about some of the students with whom I have worked--a time of reflection. I recently had the experience of attending a high school graduation for a member of my family. When I put these two experiences together and think about the changes I have seen, I am reminded of the expression, "you can't see the forest for the trees." That is, it is difficult to see the changes on a day to day basis, but when you sit back, all at once the results are there. It is not unlike watching a tree grow. Even though it is not apparent, the tree grows all winter long. It is not until the buds appear that we "see" the growth and then it seems as if overnight the tree is in full leaf. This seems to apply to some of the students I have worked with. I wonder if anything is taking place and then they seem to come into full bloom.

I did some landscaping at home this year and I almost cut out one bush. I was sure it was dead. Thanks to the frequent spring rains, I didn't get around to cutting it down. One morning I went out and it was in full bloom. That reminded me of my students. They don't always grow according to my time schedule! I need to remind myself to respect their own pattern of growth, and not to impose my schedule on them. I know that many of the young people I work with will not bloom until a year or two after they graduate. My goal is to have the patience "to watch the tree grow" even if I don't get to witness the blooming.

Counseling is like . . . Opening a letter.

Students come to us in all stages of readiness for counseling. There are some who, the minute they come in the office, begin to spill out everything on their minds. Others are more reluctant to tell us what is going on. With these students we must be careful to allow them the time to be comfortable with us to the point where they are willing to invite us into a part of their lives. Depending on the student and the counselor, this could be a short time or a long time. An important factor in this is whether the students perceive us as open and willing to accept their secrets without judgment.

The analogy of "Counseling is like opening a letter," helps us to appreciate the difficulties some students have in allowing us to become a part of their secret world. As we respect them, they will find it easier to allow us to "read their letters."

Recently, I wrote a very long letter to a friend, pouring out my feelings, thoughts, and ideas, on a variety of personal issues. The day after I mailed the letter, I found a page that had gotten separated from the original letter. I sent it with a note apologizing that I had not numbered the pages. My friend would have to figure out where the page should be in the letter. I was struck by the similarity between my letter and some of the students with whom I work.

The student is like a letter, personal and confidential. A letter may have many pages, or a few, and the pages may or may not be numbered. Depending on the number of envelopes, they might be delivered at one time or separately. There seems to be an infinite variety of conditions the letter could be in when it arrives, beginning with the envelope.

The letter is protected by an envelope that must be opened before the letter can be read. Some students are more highly defended than others, their envelopes more tightly sealed. They not only moisten all the glue completely when sealing the flap, but fasten it with sealing wax as well! Others may moisten just the tip of the flap or just tuck it in. Some may just slip the letter in, but leave the flap of the envelope open. However, only when the letter is out of the envelope can you know the contents.

Until the letter is out of the envelope, it can not be read. When the letter is opened, the "secrets" are out. Sometimes the contents of a letter are so painful that only small parts can be read at a time . The letter must be put back in the envelope until a later time when, once again, it can be taken out and more of it read. You also don't know how long it took to write the letter. Was it written all at once, or did it take several days (or years) to develop?

In working with a student, we may need to meet more than once to allow the envelope to be opened. With others, the minute they sit down, the contents "come tumbling out." Once the student begins to open up, it is important to encourage them to reveal that with which they are comfortable. I have worked with some who spend the first session getting to know me, to find out how accepting I might be to what they have to say. I feel this is the time both parties begin to have an appreciation of how we will work together. Will I respect the student enough to allow time to open up? Will the student develop that sense of trust which will allow that to happen?

As a student exposes more of the "secrets," it is sometimes necessary to retreat into a safe place for a while. The key is to help the student find that safe place where she can feel secure, but still be available to feelings.

Sometimes when the counselor believes the student has found a safe place, the student will still retreat to the point of closing up completely. This is where the counselor must be patient and sensitive in helping the student "open up the envelope" again to reveal the contents. Hopefully, having once been "out of the envelope" it will be easier to come out again.

The counselor must be cognizant that it took a while to write the letter, so that it will take time to reveal the contents. The counselor's job is to help the student understand this as well.

As the two work together to read the letter, there will be pleasant surprises within which the student can learn to appreciate that the contents of the letter can help her grow.

CHAPTER EIGHT

ENDINGS

An important part of the counseling relationship is the ending of that relationship. Many times the relationship may have ended and the counselor doesn't even know it. This happens when the student chooses not to come back and doesn't let the counselor know. It could also happen when the student moves and doesn't have the opportunity to say goodbye. When this happens, counselors can only deal with their own unfinished business from the relationship as best as possible.

On the other hand, there are many times when it is obvious that counseling has come to an end and some type of closure could be helpful. The following analogies attempt to address these issues.

Ending counseling is like . . . Closing a door.

It would be difficult to say which is the most important time in counseling, if indeed, one could determine that. We know that the initial session will determine whether or not the student returns. What happens in the following sessions is in many ways the meat of the counseling. I believe that the ending of the counseling relationship is equally important. Perhaps not as much attention is paid to this since many times the student just disappears rather than having a formal ending. Having said that, I believe that we must do our best to anticipate this behavior so that we are in a position to bring closure to our work with the students. There are as many reasons as there are students as to why we don't always have an ending session. In spite of this, I think we need to be aware of the importance of that closing session. We may also need to look at ourselves and our ability to say goodbye.

In the analogy about closing a door, I address the issue of closure and how to approach it in a way that will be helpful for students to see beyond the ending into what the future may hold for them. I believe that every beginning has an ending and every ending has a beginning and we need to teach that.

The termination of counseling sessions is like passing through a door. The student-counselor relationship changes as both pass into the final stages of counseling. With this change they outgrow their original chamber.

They will move through the doorway and close the door on that part of the process.

Once through that door, the student may choose to move into newer, larger rooms-- alone. In so doing, the student may, at some point, desire the guidance and support of the counselor again. But never again will they be in that same place where they first began. There may be new rooms that they share, but they can never go back to the beginning.

Closing that door is an important step. You should take time to look back over the room, to recall what it was like, and how the student has outgrown it. Take a few minutes to walk through and experience its familiarity, touching a picture here, a piece of furniture there. A final examination of the room is an important way to say goodbye to this place before moving on.

There may be several things left unfinished. These could be tidied up before leaving and closing the door. Or, they may be taken into the next room, or they may be left undone. This leave-taking time is a decision making time about those things that are yet undone.

At the threshold, plans should be made on where to go next. While closing the door to the past, the student is moving into the future.

Plans for those first steps into new surroundings can give the student a greater sense of confidence in the ability to move on alone.

Saying goodbye is always an important part of moving into hello. Pass through the door, close it gently, and say goodbye.

At the end of an ocean cruise there is always a farewell party. At the end of a counseling relationship, the termination of that relationship is very much like the end of a cruise, and it needs to be marked with some kind of farewell "celebration."

The counseling relationship is unique from relationships in the "real world." Just like relationships develop on a cruise, intimacy develops with strangers in an unreal environment that will often terminate at the end of the cruise. Yet what has transpired between the persons in that relationship is very real and very significant. Like persons on a cruise, the counselor and students may never see each other again, and even if they do, the circumstances will never be the same.

Like a farewell party, termination in counseling has three basic ingredients: 1. review; 2. plans for the future; 3. time to say unsaid things, finish issues where possible and appropriate.

The element of true celebration is also important. There is much to celebrate; the relationship, the progress, the successes, and the hope for the future.

Saying goodbye, though often painful, is an important part of closure, releasing both parties to let go and move on. The end is also the beginning.

Ending counseling is . . . Saying goodbye to a unique experience.

In 1983 I had the opportunity to do a program with Outward Bound in Maine. I spent 10 days with 11 people whom I had not met before the trip. The setting was such that, during this time period, most of us became quite close and among the entire group there developed a sense of care and concern. We shared some trying experiences, as well as some pleasant ones. We lived in very close quarters for this time period and, as a result, got to know quite a bit about each other. At the end of the trip, we had a closing ceremony in which we attempted to bring closure to the experience. The likelihood of any of us getting together again was very slim, so it was important for us to say goodbye. Along with the sense of loss at saying goodbye, was also a sense of celebration for doing what we had done. Each person took away from the experience some very personal feelings of accomplishment, and a sense of self that was not present before the trip.

I believe there is a parallel in counseling. The counselor and the student come together, usually meeting for the first time in the counseling hour. As they spend time together they share many experiences, some painful and some joyful. At the end of their time together, it is important to have a closing ceremony, a goodbye, to bring closure to their meetings. This is a time for reflecting on what has taken place, on the experiences shared, on the expression of the feelings which have developed. It is also a time to say goodbye, to bring closure to this part of their lives, so that each is free to move on to new people and new experiences. The closing ceremony gives each the opportunity to reflect on what each has experienced during their time together--to express the growth each has seen taking place. It is an opportunity for the counselor to underscore the growth of the student, to help the student recognize and accept the sense of self that has developed during the counseling experience.

Sometimes this closing ceremony is

celebrated by both parties and is seen as a very positive experience. Sometimes there is a tendency on the part of the student to want to hang on to the counselor, and the counseling, after it is no longer appropriate to do so.

In my experience I have found that some students are afraid to trust what they have learned. They are so fearful of not being able to develop the same close relationship with another outside of counseling. Yet, if growth is to take place, the student needs to experience close, caring relationships outside of the counselor's office. As a counselor, when you encounter a student who is reluctant to say goodbye, it is very difficult to terminate the counseling relationship. Yet it must be done. To do otherwise would be harmful to the student and to the relationship.

A word of caution should be noted here. When you are in the process of discussing leftover issues, you must be careful that this is not used as a means to prolong counseling. If it appears that there are many unresolved issues, then it might be appropriate to renegotiate additional counseling sessions. It is also important to help the student understand that one does not need to wait until all issues are resolved before counseling is terminated. One continues to grow beyond the counseling sessions. The student takes the learning that has taken place and applies that learning to new situations. As in a travel experience, it is not possible to do and see all that you would like to see in the allotted time, therefore you plan additional trips. These additional trips may be in the same format as before or, they may take on different characteristics. As in counseling, future growth may take place in a variety of settings, and all could be outside the counseling format. Saying goodbye frees up the individual to consider other possibilities for growth. With the goodbye, they also should celebrate what the individual has accomplished.

Ending counseling is like . . .Tying off a loom.

When the end of counseling comes, it is important to help students understand that there is a "life beyond counseling." At this stage, they tend to focus on the ending rather than appreciate that the ending is an ending to only one phase of their life and that it also marks a beginning of the next stage.
Another phenomenon is the belief that now that they are ending counseling, all problems are solved. It is important to understand that counseling is a part of growth

and that growth continues throughout life. The student needs to see life as an ongoing, changing pattern of growth. We build on the past which helps us to be open to the future.

I believe that the analogy on weaving deals with the issue of understanding their past as a way of impacting upon their future. To understand that they are not paralyzed with what has gone on before. With some thought and creativity, they are able to change the patterns of their lives and to shape it in a way that will be more meaningful to them.

When you are going to make something on a loom, you must first warp the loom. Because this is a time consuming process, most weavers put enough yarn on the loom to make several items--like dish towels. Once this is done, you thread the bobbin with the weft thread and begin to weave. You can control the pattern in a variety of ways. One way is to use more than one shuttle, with different colors on each shuttle. Another way is to use a variegated yarn. In addition to this control, how you use the treadles also affects the pattern that you weave. Different combinations produce different results. In theory, you can warp enough yarn to make, perhaps 10 dish towels, each with a different pattern.

When you have made one towel as long as you want, you leave several inches of warp for fringe before you begin the next towel. You also have an option of making the towels different sizes. When you have completed the weaving, it is necessary to tie off the warp so that it doesn't become unraveled. As you take the towels off the loom, it is necessary to cut between each towel and tie that yarn off as well.

In thinking about weaving and students, we have a parallel. The warp for the student is the family. Each member of the family is usually a different weft thread, so that each is a unique individual. In addition, the people the student encounters as she leaves the family and moves on to other experiences, also contributes to the weft. As the student grows, because of life changes, the treadle . patterns can change as well. We seldom go through life with the same patterns with which we started. There will be growth spurts and what might seem to be plateaus, so there will be spaces in our growth patterns.

When a student comes into counseling it is usually due to some problem with the pattern that has been woven. The counselor's job is to help the student learn how to weave a different pattern in life. Most of the time, when the student leaves counseling, it is not necessary to cut apart the various stages of her growth. Rather, the student has learned how to make a pattern that fits. At the end of counseling, it is important to tie off the loose ends so that the student doesn't become unraveled and revert to a pattern that is less healthy.

Ending counseling is like . . . Finding answers within yourself.

Have you ever thought about what the purpose of counseling is? Seems like a strange question to ask counselors! Yet, I believe it is an important question to consider. The obvious answers are there--to help students learn how to cope, to help them get over a crises, to help them grow, etc. Is there something beyond the obvious? I think so. I believe that one of our major goals is to work ourselves out of a job. To help students in such a way that they no longer need us. It is important for us to teach students skills they can continue to use beyond counseling. Through counseling we can help them develop a sense of confidence so that they can figure out things for themselves. The analogy of answers within yourself addresses this issue of one of the goals of counseling.

I recently read a book, <u>Plain</u> <u>and</u> <u>Simple</u> by Sue Bender, in which she talks about living with an Amish family in Iowa. She went into considerable detail of what this experience was like for her, as one of the "English" (what the Amish call non-Amish people). She observed their lifestyle and how they were able to live a simple life. A feature which stood out for her, was the tremendous cooperation among the Amish families in the area. How they were able to live without, what the English consider, the necessities of life which resulted in a relatively stress-free non-cluttered life. The time came when she had to leave this family and go back to her own family. She left with many unanswered questions about herself.

Sometime later, she asked an Amish family in Holmes County, Ohio if she might come stay with them for a while. This family constellation was quite different from the family she lived with in Iowa. In some ways, because she had been in correspondence with the Ohio family, she was included in more of their activities. Once again, it came time for her to return to her own family. This time many of her questions about herself were answered, even though she still had many unanswered questions. At this point, she had a breakthrough and realized she no longer needed to go live with the Amish to find her answers, she had them within herself. She had learned that what she needed to do was to provide the space in her own life, so that she would be able to find the answers.

Students come to counseling, seeking answers about many things. Whether they find the answers depends on their level of maturity, their openness to finding answers, and if they are asking the right questions. I have had students who would come in their freshman year, go away, and return again in a later year, still looking for answers, but better able to ask the appropriate questions. If we have worked well together, the student begins to realize that the answers lie within. My job has been to teach that. When the end to counseling comes, I hope that the student leaves with the knowledge of how to go about finding the answers. This tacit knowledge is a part of all of us, if we would only learn to trust it. Part of the growth that takes place in the counseling environment is that the student learns to look within for answers. I see this learning as part of the process of bringing closure to the counseling sessions.

CHAPTER 9

WHERE DO YOU GO FROM HERE?

> Not knowing already how and what to do, practice
> feeling (life) out of what is not known through the
> warmth and anxiety, not sticking to a particular
> way even though it is quite good open to feeling the
> various possibilities, the tentative ways of giving
> life to our life . . . the mystery is that is it possible
> to do what we don't know how to do.
>
> Tassajara Cooking

In the proceeding chapters I have attempted to show how human language can be used to develop a narrative and/or stories in the creation of personal realities. With a greater appreciation of metaphorical features of knowing and meaning, we can use metaphors as a vehicle for communication and change to aid the organization of personal experiences in our students.

I have tried to challenge you to think in new ways about how to interact with students. Now it is up to you. Hopefully this book has given you some new ways of thinking about counseling.

Using the analogy of cooking and

counseling as suggested above, once more listen to the Tassajara

> Begin and continue with what is in front of you. . . the way to be a cook is to cook. (The way to be a counselor is to counsel.) The results don't have to be just right, measuring up to some imagined or ingrained taste. Our cooking doesn't have to prove how wonderful or talented we are. Our original worth is not something which can be measured, increased or decreased. Just feed, satisfy, nourish. Enter each activity thoroughly, freshly, vitally. Splash! There is completely no secret: just plunging in, allowing time, making space, giving energy, tending each situation with warmhearted effort. The spoon, the knife, the food, the hunger; broken plates and broken plans Play, don't work. Work it out.
>
> (Brown, p. 1)

How eloquently that speaks of counseling.

Counseling is an art and,

> You follow recipes, you listen to advice, you go your own way. Even wholehearted effort sometimes falls short, the best intentions do not insure success. There is no help for it, so go ahead, begin and continue: with yourself, with others, with vegetables.
>
> (Brown, p. 1)

REFERENCES

Barker, P. (1985). Using metaphors in psychotherapy. New York: Brunner/Mazel

Brown, E. (1973). Tassajara cooking. Colorado: Shambhala.

Bender, S.(1989). Plain and simple. San Franciso: Harper.

Bugental, J. (1992) The art of the psychotherapist. New York: Norton.

Cirillo, L., Crider, C. Distinctive therapeutic uses of metaphor. In *Psychotherapy.* 32/Winter 1995, N0. 4.

Combs, G., Freedman, J. (1990). Symbol story & ceremony. New York: W.W. Norton & Company.

Frantz, R. The use of metaphor and fantasy as an additional exploration of awareness. In *The Gestalt Journal,* VI, 2, pg. 29.

Glasser, W. (1985). Positive addiction. New York: Harper & Row.

Glasser, W.(1965) Reality therapy. New York: Harper & Row.

Gordon, D. (1978). Therapeutic metaphors. Cupertino, CA: META Publications.

Gruber, E. (programer). (1967). Miller Analogy Test (MAT). NY: Araco.

Kopp, R. (1995). Metaphor therapy: using client-generated metaphors in psychotherapy. New York: Brunner/Mazel.

Kopp, R., Craw. J. Metaphoric language, metaphoriac cognition, and cognitive therapy in *Psychotherapy,* 35, Fall 1998, 3.

Lee, R. (1999). Therapeutic Chaos. In Richard Lee (Ed.) *CHI*, No. 81. San Clemente, CA: China Healthways Institute.

Piper, W., Haunan G. (1976). The Little Engine That Could. New York: Platt & Munk.

Rogers, C. (1951). Client-centered therapy. Boston: Houghton Mifflin

Rusk & Read (1988). I want to change but I don't know how. Los Angeles: Price Stern, and Sloan.

Satir, V. (1972). Peoplemaking. Palo Alto, CA: Science and Behavior Books.

Webster's New World Dictionary, (2nd ed.) (1976). Cleveland, OH: Wm Collins & World Publication Co. Inc.

Woolf, R. (1940). *Aladin and the Wonderful Lamp* . pp. 94-112 **In   Edrick Vredenburg (Ed.).** Children's Stories from the Arabian Nights London: Raphael Tuck & Sons, Ltd.

SUGGESTED READINGS

Angus, L. (1996). Metaphoric expressiveness within the psychotherapeutic relationship: a qualitative analysis. (doctoral dissertation, York University) Ottawa: National Library of Canada.

Barker, P. (1996). Psychotherapeutic metaphors: a guide to theory and practice. New York: Brunner/Mazel.

Barker, P. (1985). Using metaphors in psychotherapy. New York: Brunner/Mazel.

Close, H. (1998). Metaphor in psychotherapy: clinical applications of stories and allegories. San Luis Obispo, Calif.: Impact Publishers.

Combs, G., Freedman, J. (1990). Symbol, story, and ceremony: using metaphor in individual and family therapy: New York: Norton.

Cox, M., Theilgaard, A. (1987). Mutative metaphors in psychotherapy: the aeolian mode. (1987). London; New York: Tavistock Publications.

deShazer, S., Kral, R. vol. eds. (1986). Indirect approaches in therapy. *Family therapy collections;* 19, Rockville, MD.: Aspen Publishers.

Erickson, M. (1982). My voice will go with you. Sidney Rosen (Ed.). NY: Norton.

Faulkner, C. (1994). Metaphors of identity [cassette recording]. Lyons: Genesis II.

Freeman, J., Epston, D., Lobovits,D. (1997). Playful approaches to serious problems: narrative therapy with children and their families. New York: W. W. Norton.

Freedman, J., Combs, G. (1996) Narrative therapy: the social construction of preferred realities. New York: Norton.

Gersie, A., King, N. (1990). Storymaking in education and therapy. London: Kingsley.

Grove, D., Panzer, B. (1989) Resolving traumatic memories: metaphors and symbols in psychotherapy. New York: Irvington Publishers.

Haley, J., (1973) Uncommon therapy: the psychiatric techniques of Milton Erickson. NY: Norton.

Lankton, C., Lankton, S, (1989) Tales of enchantment: goal-oriented metaphors for adults and children in therapy. New York: Brunner/Mazel.

Lyddon, W.,Clay, A., & Sparks, C.., Metaphor and Change In Counseling, *Journal of Counseling & Development,* Summer 2001, 79, p. 269-274.

Mills, J., Crowley, R. in collaboration with Margaret Ryan. (1986). Therapeutic metaphors for children and the child within. New York: Brunner/Mazel.

Monk, G., [et al.] ed. (1997). Narrative therapy in practice: the archaeology of hope. San Francisco: Jossey-Bass.

Pearce, S. (1996). Flash of insight: metaphor and narrative therapy. Boston: Allyn and Bacon.

Rico, G.(1983). Writing the natural way. Los Angeles, CA. J. P.

Tarcher. Siegelman, Ellen. (1990). Metaphor and meaning in psychotherapy. New York: Guilford Press.

Wubbolding, R. (1991). Understanding reality therapy: a metaphorical approach. New York, N.Y.: Harper Perennial.

ISBN 141200526-4

9 781412 005265